BENEDETTO CROCE:
COLLECTED WORKS

Volume 7

POLITICS AND MORALS

POLITICS AND MORALS

BENEDETTO CROCE

Routledge
Taylor & Francis Group

LONDON AND NEW YORK

First published in 1946 by George Allen & Unwin Ltd

This edition first published in 2019
by Routledge
2 Park Square, Milton Park, Abingdon, Oxon OX14 4RN

and by Routledge
52 Vanderbilt Avenue, New York, NY 10017

Routledge is an imprint of the Taylor & Francis Group, an informa business

© 1946 Benedetto Croce

British Library Cataloguing in Publication Data
A catalogue record for this book is available from the British Library

ISBN: 978-0-367-10994-3 (Set)
ISBN: 978-0-429-05271-2 (Set) (ebk)
ISBN: 978-0-367-14360-2 (Volume 7) (hbk)
ISBN: 978-0-367-14370-1 (Volume 7) (pbk)
ISBN: 978-0-429-03160-1 (Volume 7) (ebk)

Publisher's Note
The publisher has gone to great lengths to ensure the quality of this reprint but points out that some imperfections in the original copies may be apparent.

Disclaimer
The publisher has made every effort to trace copyright holders and would welcome correspondence from those they have been unable to trace.

BENEDETTO CROCE

POLITICS AND
MORALS

Translated from the Italian
by
Salvatore J. Castiglione

LONDON
GEORGE ALLEN & UNWIN LTD

BOOK
PRODUCTION
WAR ECONOMY
STANDARD

*Produced in complete conformity
with the authorized economy
standards*

PRINTED IN GREAT BRITAIN

in 11 point Baskerville type

BY BRADFORD & DICKENS
LONDON, W.C. 1

CONTENTS

Chapter I

ELEMENTS OF POLITICS

I. POLITICAL SENSE

WHEN we speak of political sense we think immediately of the perception of convenience, of expediency, of reality, of suitability, and the like. People who act or who judge the actions of others in accordance with this perception are said to be endowed with political sense. On the other hand, those who behave contrary to expediency, even though they may be full of the best moral intentions and may be kindled by the noblest ideals, are thought to be lacking in political sense.

In the face, therefore, of what we might call this everyday admission, it is irrational to object to the doctrine that political action is only an action guided by the sense of what is useful and directed toward a utilitarian goal, and that *per se* it cannot be qualified as either moral or immoral.

Perhaps the motive for opposing particularly this last proposition is to be found in the unconscious substitution that we are accustomed to make of the concept of what is for our self-interest for the concept of what is useful—in spite of Aristotle's warning against confusing love of oneself with evil love of oneself, and the whole development of modern thought and the many disciplines relating to routine behaviour which inculcate this difference and justify the concept of what is useful.

Although this erroneous substitution has hindered or weakened the serious study of politics, by doing away with the character of politics as distinct from ethics, since the living reality of politics cannot be denied, the substitution has

led to the treatment of what is merely political as a thing
from which no one can abstain completely, even though not
infrequently it is more or less immoral.   Thus a dualism is set
up between political action and moral action.   A consequence
of this dualism is the common opinion that politics is a sad
necessity (an opinion to which some philosophers have given
an important place in the forefront of their speculations,
making of politics and of the State a temporary expedient and
a transitory condition of mankind).   Another consequence is
the series of illogical maxims which declare that it is sometimes
necessary to do evil in order to attain good, that private ethics
are different from public ethics, that it is impossible to take
part in politics and keep one's hands clean, and that in the
interest of the State one must, if necessary, break a promise
or commit murders.   These maxims are illogical because our
human conscience cries out to us that in no case is it permissible to break a promise or commit murders; that there is
not one set of ethics in the home and another in the public
square; that one cannot do evil in order to attain good, as
though evil and good were merchandise to be exchanged;
that our hands must be kept clean; that the quality of the
means must not conflict with the quality of the end.   Worse
than illogical, these maxims would be called degraded if we
did not recall that they are sometimes found on the lips of
such men as Frederick of Prussia and Camillo di Cavour;
and in such cases they express the genuine anguish that is
experienced in performing actions for which a rational
necessity is felt.   And yet these actions cannot be set into the
schemes of the doctrines professed; indeed, their very
authors turn away from them after having performed them,
and apprehensively acknowledge their guilt, or attribute the
sole responsibility for their deeds to God, who has put them
in such straits that they have had to do what they have done.

But the truth is that if, at a time when the moral conscience was at its greatest clarity, the performance of these actions proved necessary (necessary, of course, not to satisfy one's own lust for power or other private ambitions or passions, and not because of the habit of brutality and evil-doing, but for the sacred protection, for the development, or for the rebirth of the fatherland), these actions can be neither a breach of promise, nor murder, nor any kind of roguery or wickedness; just as the " magnanimous lie " of which Tasso speaks could not be a " lie," exactly because it was " magnanimous," except as a poetic metaphor.

Not only is political action any action which is useful, but the concept of political action is co-extensive with that of useful action. Nor will we ever be in a position to adduce any characteristics which may distinguish political action within the category of useful action. If political ability is necessary to govern the State or to lead a party, it is likewise necessary to rule one's own family, to establish and cultivate relationships of love and friendship; and it is even necessary toward the animals we use and toward things, granted that things, too, obey laws and in their own way (or according to the theory of Campanella) have life and feeling. Therefore, in speaking, as here, of politics and of political actions we mean simply to turn our attention to certain facts which are ordinarily quite important and frequently offer material for research and discussion. It would not be possible to define these facts by logic within the infinite expanse of that which is useful. We shall refer to them according to the ideas commonly connoted by the word " politics."

It is useless to try, as is frequently done, to single out political actions from among practical and utilitarian actions, as those which have to do with the life of the State. After all, what is the State? It is nothing but a series of useful actions performed by a group of persons or by individual members within a group. For this reason this series of actions is not to be distinguished from any other series performed by any other group or by any other individual; for the individual is never isolated and always lives in some form of social relationship. Nor is anything to be gained by defining the State as an entity made up of institutions or laws, because there is no social group or individual that does not possess its own institutions and ways of life, and which is not subject to laws and regulations. Strictly speaking, every form of life is, in this sense, fundamentally like that of the State. Therefore, in speaking of the State as something specific, we mean likewise to refer to the general connotation of the word.

If the concept of State has no value in distinguishing political actions from other utilitarian actions, it has even less value in contrast with individual actions or as an entity with its own life above and beyond individuals. The attempt to give this concept some such connotation is the usual trick played, through the use of metaphorical language, by the failure to think, and clinched by rhetorical emphasis. The idea of the State is subject to this trick as are other abstractions, such as Truth, Good and Beauty, capitalized and suspended on high as bright stars. From this way of reasoning arise the absurd questions as to what Truth, Good and Beauty are, objectively and in themselves, and the absurd theories which explain how man behaves with regard to those ideas, how he learns them, imitates them and puts them into practice, or how he betrays them and revolts against them. Finally, dissatisfaction with such doctrines develops and leads to the realization that there exists not Truth, but the thought which thinks; not Good, but moral volition; not Beauty, but poetic and artistic activity; not the State, but political actions. However, the word " State," to which the Italians of the Renaissance gave a political significance, seems almost a paradoxical word because it brings the idea of something static into political life, which, like any other form of life, is dynamic or, better, spiritually dialectical.

The word " State " is meant to indicate all the institutions, customs and laws which govern the actions of man, and more precisely the whole body of fundamental and constitutional laws. In the first place, however, laws themselves are merely the actions of individuals; they represent the will of individuals asserting itself to promote certain more or less general tendencies which are deemed useful. In the second place, inasmuch as these tendencies are indicated only abstractly by laws, their translation into action is not merely a matter of obedience or imitation on the part of each individual, but the individual's real creation, laws playing the role of a simple material element, that is negative in the formal synthesis. In other words, it is known that laws are important; but far more important is the manner in which they are observed, that is, the actual behaviour of man. It is also known that laws, when interpreted and put into effect, become broad, flexible, richer; in a word, they change. Exactly for this reason, the distinction between State and government, very common in political doctrines and debates, but of little practical importance, cannot be accepted in the realm of pure theory, that is, of pure truth. For those who seek concreteness rather than abstractions, the State is nothing but the government and assumes complete reality in the government; outside the unbroken chain of the actions of the government there remains only the principle of the abstract necessity of these same actions and the assumption that the laws have an unchanging value of their own, different from the actions performed in their light or in their shadow.

However, this is one of those truths that with some reason

are called " dangerous," in so far as they are easily used to
defend or justify certain unpraiseworthy actions and measures.
Thus the critical theory that grammar is devoid of truth and
consists of abstract and arbitrary rules might be cheerfully
welcomed by the ungrammatical schoolboy, whereas the real
meaning of this theory is that grammar must be studied
because it is useful and that it makes use of abstractions in
order to be useful, and for no other purpose.   The abstract-
ness of laws and the concreteness which the State secures only
in the act of government do not mean that institutions, customs and laws are to be disregarded and despised, and that
one should, if it were possible, rule from day to day and from
hour to hour, improvising short-lived laws for each occasion.
Nor do they mean that, inasmuch as normal life is an
unending revolution, one should engage in revolutionary acts
at every moment.   This deduction would be a convenient
sophism, based, like all sophisms, on a play on words and a
subtle substitution of one class of ideas for another.

In spite of their abstract nature, laws have been and still
are indispensable.   With reason, they are hailed, in the words
of Aristotle, as " intellect without greed," that is, as the
creation of man's own will which he pledges not to touch or
disturb with his interests and desires.   Everyone desires laws,
lasting laws, so that he may be able to plan his future according to a pattern which, though altered by events, will be
effective.   The relative stability of laws is what we call
" peace," so dear to the heart of every industrious man.   The
force and appeal of tradition and of the past are founded on
institutions, laws and customs.   On the other hand, governments not founded on any right, but arbitrarily created do not
grow any roots, or if they do, grow them very slowly and
with difficulty.   The ancient peoples praised especially legislators, founders and reformers of States; because, if men of

war and diplomacy stand for strength of action in the present, for victories, conquests and the security of States against dangers and ruin, legislators stand for the preservation and increase of these advantages in the future by means of the institutions which guarantee them. Polemics and satire against the so-called " bigoted supporters " of the laws and against the " Vestals " of the institutions may have some justification in that superstitious timidity which sometimes interferes with the active life of the State. The other polemic against the legal formalists has some justification against pedantry and superficiality which, by having recourse to abstractions, prevent a view of the reality of historical events and of accomplished, irrevocable changes. Greater blame, perhaps, is deserved by those who lack the sense of tradition, of continuity and of legality even though they work eagerly on behalf of the good that is necessarily unstable and shallow in so far as it is based solely on the arbitrary decision of the individual. If the former group can be charged with a deficiency of political sense, this latter group is certainly deficient in juridical sense, which is also a special form of political sense.

In apparent contradiction to the theory that the essence of the State is only political action, and that political actions are useful actions, stands the widely accepted view that the origin and the government of the State are to be attributed to force. At first sight, this view seems to be the direct opposite of the theory of usefulness and economic convenience, or at least quite different from it. In this connection an eclectic attempt has been made to combine these two contradictory conceptions by relating force or violence to the origin of States and the idea of utilitarian convenience to their life and development. At this point it is worth remarking that the " birth " or " origin " referred to in these and in similar cases is not at all a historical fact, but, rather, the origin, the birth, the eternal nature or idea of the State; and consequently there is no place for a historical distinction between origin and development and between primitive and later times. As was known and stated by the ancients, man is by nature a social or political being; and, as we moderns say, the State is not a fact, but a spiritual category. Another caution: we must not limit the idea of force to the superficial meaning which the word usually suggests—almost the seizing of a man by the neck, bending him and forcing him to the ground, and similar meanings. But we must think of force in the complete sense of all human and spiritual force, which includes the wisdom of the intellect no less than the strength of the arm, foresight and prudence no less than daring and boldness, gentleness no less than severity, candour no less than discernment or even malice, the virtue of beauty no less than the beauty of virtue.

If the concept of force is correctly understood in this sense, it follows that one cannot conceive of force as distributed in such a way that, in a large group of men one or a few possess it and the others do not, or that one or a few possess more of it than others, so that that one or those few should impose their will on the others and dominate them. The varied distribution of that force is not quantitative but qualitative. It is a variety of tendencies, abilities and virtues; each one of these seeks its complement in the others, each one needs the others, each one can in reciprocal fashion impose itself upon the others, threaten to deprive them of its own support, or, as we say, exert pressure on the others. And the result of these different pressures is the agreement on a way of living, the reciprocal accord. The dilemma as to whether the State is founded on force or mutual consent and the question as to which is the legitimate State, that founded on force or only that founded on consent, are problems on a par with the distinction already made between State and government. Actually, in the field of politics, force and consent are correlative terms, and one does not exist without the other. The objection will be raised that this is a " forced " consent. But every consent is more or less forced; that is, every consent is based on the " force " of certain facts and is, therefore, " conditioned." If the *de facto* condition changes, the consent, as is natural, is withdrawn, debates and struggles break out, and a new consent is established on the new condition. There is no political body which escapes this vicissitude: in the most liberal State as in the most oppressive tyranny there is always a consent, and it is always forced, conditioned, changeable. Otherwise, neither the State nor the life of the State would exist.

Expressing the same idea in other words, we may designate by the term " authority " everything included in the concept of force, whether it be promise or threat, reward or punishment; and by the term "liberty" everything connoted by the concept of spontaneity and agreement. It will then be seen that in every State authority and liberty are inseparable. (And this is equally true of the extremes of despotism and liberalism.) Liberty struggles against authority, yet desires it; and authority checks liberty, yet keeps it alive or awakens it, because neither would exist without the other. We exalt liberty, and rightly so. What other word so warms the heart of man? None is so powerful except, perhaps, the word love. In a way, the connotations of the two words merge; because liberty, like love, is life that desires to expand and enjoy itself; life in all its forms, felt by each one in his own way in that infinite variety, in that individuality of tendencies and of activities of which the unity of the universe is woven. And by " liberty " here we mean nothing more than this joy of

doing, this joy of living, the natural faculty of man to do what
is pleasing to him, not the moral liberty usually perceived by
the stern moralists, who, with their "moral liberty," are
capable of misrepresenting even the simple impulses and con-
fidences of Romeo and Juliet! But with reason, too, we
praise authority, order, regularity, the sacrifice which individuals and groups owe to each other and which implies
the strengthening of any individual in every other, and of each
one in every one else. Whereas the word "liberty" is pleasing,
the word "authority" is chilling to the spirit. The fault lies
solely with those who praise exclusively either force or
authority, either consent or liberty, and forget that the term
excluded by them is already included in the one they have
accepted, because it is its correlative. The practical politician
agrees with Joseph De Maistre that it is necessary to preach
the benefits of authority to the people and those of liberty to
the princes.

We do not deny that in the arguments favouring liberty
against authority, and vice versa, and the principle of consent against the principle of force, and vice versa, as in the
other arguments in favour of the State against the government, quite important matters are often the subject of discussion, almost *per speculum et in aenigmate*. But they are
matters which concern historical and contingent situations and
which pertain to the emotions and interests of the citizens of
a given State at a given time. Later, because of philosophical
immaturity and sometimes as a result of oratorical ability or
polemic violence, these matters are elevated to the position of
supreme concepts or to the position of derivations and deduc-
tions from those supreme concepts, thus giving the value of
concepts to metaphors used in the discussion and transforming
problems of practical politics into theoretical problems.

Furthermore, we do not deny that to define sovereignty

and to find the person or persons in whom, according to the various types of State, sovereignty is embodied may be matters of practical meaning and importance. On the other hand, in the realm of pure theory such a definition certainly has no place and such a search no meaning. As long as all degrees of force are thought of as one concept, varying only with respect to the degree found in the components of the State, it is logical to define sovereignty as the possession of force, of the greatest force, and to seek out wherein it lies, according to the different types of States. Once the concept of qualitative differentiation has been substituted for the above inaccurate concept, it is just as logical to reach the conclusion that in a State every one is by turn sovereign and subject. Not even kings escape such a law: many a time they have complained openly of their "lack of freedom," of that freedom enjoyed by even men of the lowest rank, men who have nothing, have no ambitions, and are indifferent to praise or blame (like the punchinellos of the second part of *Faust*). In the relationship between ruler and ruled sovereignty belongs to neither but to the relationship itself. In truth, when we are forced to find it in something which surpasses and dominates the relation itself, we are tempted to answer that the sovereign is God or Idea or History (*omnis potestas a Deo*), that is, we are tempted to change this meaningless question to one with meaning. If sovereignty exists in every part of the relation, *nec cubat in ulla*, the division of States according to the persons who exercise the sovereignty also collapses as devoid of theoretic value, and with it collapses above all the famous tripartition into monarchy, aristocracy and democracy. This tripartition retains a certain philosophical meaning, not in relation to the place to be assigned to sovereignty, but in so far as it perceives three phases of all political life: collaboration, which is for all; advice, which is for the few, the optimates

B

or aristocrats; and resolution, which is for one individual. Taken in this meaning, however, the tripartition would indicate the organic composition of any State, that is, of the State in the abstract, rather than three forms of States.

The political theories which up to now have been rejected because they are one-sided have, for this very reason, one merit at least: they are founded on a real aspect or phase and they recall it emphatically in cases where there is a tendency to forget it or deny it. But there is a political theory which does not even have such a merit, is not founded on any phase of the political relationship, and yet is the theory which boasts the greatest number of followers. This is the theory which, in order to avoid misunderstandings, we shall call neither democratic nor Jacobin, but the theory of equality. "Democracy" signifies the tendency to give the masses, that is the common people, added importance in political deliberations. And it is always more or less an empirical problem. "Jacobinism" signifies a practical attitude which departs from an abstract ideal. In order to put this ideal into effect, Jacobinism has recourse to impositions and violence. For this reason, the name "Jacobin" is given not only to the extreme democrats, but also to extreme conservatives and aristocrats, that is to say, to all who have resort to similar impositions and violence, usually of brief duration and with meagre results. In given circumstances democracy may or may not be plausible, and Jacobinism will always be very slightly plausible. But neither the one nor the other is intrinsically impossible or absurd, as is the theory of equality. This theory presupposes the equality of individuals, and places it at the foundation of States. This equality would not be conceivable except as a form of self-sufficiency, of the complete self-satisfaction of the individual, with nothing to ask of his fellow man, whose equal he is. Equality in this form cannot be of value in the founding of a State; on the contrary, it shows that the State is superfluous, since every individual is a State in himself. Not even a "contract" is possible between these independents, because there is a lack of bargaining material, that is, of that variety which is the basis of reciprocal rights and duties. In order that the State may rise according to this hypothesis it is necessary to introduce a *deus ex machina* or to have one or more individuals suddenly detach themselves from the rest, as being neither the equals of the others nor like them. This would amount to the nullification of the hypothesis and of the whole theory. We do not intend to deny the effectiveness which this theory may have had, has, and will have in the future as the myth of certain economic and moral doctrines and needs. Likewise, we do not deny that a derivative of this theory, the theory of majority rule, has value as a practical expedient and as a symbol of what is practically possible at a given moment. But, of course, in political science its falseness is complete; and when it is taken as a criterion, all good judgment of political matters runs into insurmountable obstacles and finally goes astray. The "liberty" and "fraternity" which this theory associates with the idea of "equality" are such empty terms, subject to anyone's arbitrary interpretation, that one understands the abuses hurled at these noble words by men gifted with a keen feeling for politics and history; men who, because of their hatred for these words, have become ardent partisans of "force," in a partial and approximate interpretation, that is, one might say, the force to box the ears of those who believe in those stupid formulas and of those who go about repeating them for the use of fools. In truth, is there anything more stupid than the "liberty" and the "fraternity" attributed to a row of cold, smooth billiard balls, all of the same size? This leads us to say that the theory of equality, for which there is no logical place in the political relation, has its true origin within the framework of mathematics and mechanics, both of them unable to comprehend the living world. In fact, although the theory of equality represents a mistake found in all ages and always reappearing, the period of its greatest glory was the century of mechanical discoveries.

It would seem that in the loss of political sense and judgment one could not sink any lower than the theory of equality. Yet this does happen and as a result of the very distress which that ideology awakens in the minds and in the souls of men by promising respect for equality and the abstract freedom of equality, and by violating it time after time. This occurs because every development and every conclusion of that theory, as well as every attempt to put it into practice which proceeds from such premises, alters equality and represses liberty, even though with the purpose of " compelling men to be free " (as was wittily stated by Rousseau). The only means left, then, for saving the principle of equality and liberty is the egoarchic and anarchic doctrine. This is the only theory which promises man full and complete enjoyment of liberty, even if it upsets all judgment on history as it has developed up to our time, and even if it shifts admiration from social to antisocial men. But this theory, which springs from the heart of the theory of equality, is the vengeance of daughter against mother, the criticism and irony of the theory itself, its *reductio ad absurdum*, and, like the mother theory, it cannot be called a political theory because it denies the object which it should explain.

II. The State and Ethics

In political action, in attempts to reach a definite goal, everything becomes a political means—everything, including in certain respects morality and religion, that is, moral and religious ideas, sentiments and institutions. The initial situation is given in each case : the men with whom we have to deal are always what they are; their ideas, their prejudices, their good or bad dispositions, their virtues and their defects furnish the material on which and with which we must work and there is no way of substituting for them more pleasing material. If, in order to agree with men in a common action or to induce them to come to an agreement, it is necessary to soothe their illusions, flatter their vanity, appeal to their most superstitious and childish beliefs (as, for example, the miracle of St. Gennaro), or to their most superficial or most superficially understood ideas (for example, equality, liberty and fraternity and the other so-called "principles of '89," which are big emotional realities, whatever may be their theoretical value), then it will be well to adopt these means. We must not be shocked by them. Every form of human activity, as it unfolds, takes strength from all other activities and it subjects and makes its own the products of all the other activities. It would be the same as being scandalized by the poet who uses thoughts and affections, joys and griefs, good and evil, all as material for his poetry and turns all to winged images.

But there is still another reason for not being shocked. Pure poetry does not dispel reflection, criticism and science from the spirit and from the world, but, rather, prepares for and almost summons them. Just so, politics, which is pure politics, does not destroy, but produces morality, in which it finds its completion and highest expression. In the world of reality there is no sphere of political or economic activity that can stand by itself, closed and isolated; but there is only the process of spiritual activity, in which process what is useful is continually being transformed into what is ethical.

The ethical spirit has in politics the premise of its activity and also its tool, almost as though it were a body which politics fills with renewed soul and bends to its own will. There is no moral life unless economic and political life is first established; as the ancients used to say, first the "living" and then "good living." On the other hand, there can be no moral life that is not both economic and political life, just as there can be no soul without a body. And moral man does not put into practice his morality except by acting in a political manner and by accepting the logic of politics. Quoting two letters of St. Bernard, written in the course of his spirited and varied struggle in favour of the Church against King Ruggiero of Sicily and containing, within a brief interval, two conflicting assertions, a historian points out that "that was politics, of course, but not the politics of a saint." This should be countered with the observation that it was indeed the "politics of a saint," of a saint who, in order to attain his saintly goal, availed himself of the sole means of attaining it, which were those offered him by politics. And was not protestantism itself, which contributed so greatly to the restoration of moral intimacy and sincerity, forced from the very beginning to adopt political methods and later to learn, in this connection, from its Jesuit adversaries, excellent teachers of such matters in theory and in practice?

The a-morality of politics, the priority (in time) of politics over morality, constitute its specific character and make it possible for it to serve as the instrument of moral life. But the sphere of politics is not the only one; nor is it self-sufficient. This must be pointed out so that the origin of this specific character of politics may not be misconceived or distorted into a sort of parthenogenesis and so that it may not be imagined that there can exist a political man entirely devoid of moral conscience. This would be the same as

admitting that a " political man " can exist without being a
" man." The specific always sprouts from the trunk of unity
and humanity, as a phase of a spiritual circle. Would a poet
without experience of affections, morality, and thoughts, a
cold, dull and deficient poet, be a poet? Is it not known that
poetry is the expression of a personality and that, therefore,
in order to create poetry, the first requirement is the full
development of man? Do we not laugh at those claiming to
be poets, who strive for poetry by means of stylistic efforts,
metric exercises, and notes on what their senses perceive; and
do we not advise them to turn round and go back to the roots
of being, and to create for themselves a heart and an intellect?
Similarly, a political man without experience and, consequently, without moral conscience, not only would not last
in his work and would not dedicate himself to it as one of the
highest offices, but he would also be unable to handle other
men and make use of their moral sentiments as convenient
tools. Their psychology would be unknown to him because
he would never have lived according to it. Therefore, he
could not even be what we call a " cynical political man."

But in the fields of ethics, which we have now entered, it
is no longer a question of moral and human experience,
indispensable to the purely political man; the political sphere
here has been left behind. The life lived is a moral one, for
which, as has been said, politics is a means and not an end.
Moral man is *vir bonus agendi peritus*. His moral education
calls also for political education and for the cultivation and
use of virtues which more appropriately should be called
practical, such as prudence, wisdom, patience and daring.

In this elevation of pure politics to an ethical position even
the word " State " takes on new meaning: it is no longer a
simple utilitarian relation, the synthesis of force and mutual
consent, of authority and liberty, but the incarnation of the

human ethos and therefore an ethical State or State of culture, as it is also called. And, along with the word "State"
the words "authority" and "sovereignty," which are the
authority and the sovereignty of duty and of the moral ideal,
take on new meaning. So it is with the word "liberty,"
which, in so far as it is moral liberty, cannot help being one and
the same thing with this duty and this ideal. So it is, too,
with the word "consent," which is ethical approval and
devotion to "force," but to the force of good, so that consent
is not more or less forced, but becomes full and complete,
love replaces fear, or, to put it in theological terms, there is
a transition from "law" to "grace." And new meaning is
taken on even by the word "equality," which no longer
means mathematical equality, but Christian equality before
God, whose children we all are, the low and the high; it
is the consciousness of our common humanity and of our
common rights. Because of this characteristic the ethical
State does not tolerate, either above itself or by its side, other
forms of association, all of which it must subordinate or deny
and nullify. When the Church was the opponent of the
State and was dominant, the Church was the true ethical
State; and when the temporal State undertook its struggle
with the Church, it did not cease this struggle until it had
assimilated the Church to itself, by considering itself the only
true Church, the representative of the needs of a more perfect
morality.

From this point of view, that exaltation of the State which,
begun by Hegel during the classical period of German
philosophy and repeated in Italy by Spaventa and others, still
re-echoes in many schools to-day, may seem intelligible, though
redundant. Inasmuch as the State was understood as the
moral life, as the very concreteness of moral life, it followed
precisely that it should be elevated to the heights where Kant

had placed moral law and that it should become an object
of the same reverence and veneration. But the mistake of
those theorists consisted, and still consists, in their having
conceived moral life in a form inadequate to it, namely, the
form of political life and of the State in a political sense.

The State, politically understood, that is, the State by
itself is, as we know, one and the same thing as the government; it is a relation based on authority and consent which
has as its enemies, and treats as such those who do not accept
it and intend to change it. According to circumstances, they
are called traitors, rebels, conspirators, undesirables, and they
are executed, imprisoned, exiled and persecuted and punished
in other ways. And because of the tendency which that
political relation, or state order, has and must have to preserve
its existence, it watches and suspects all free and unruly spirits,
and even critics and thinkers, who, because they centre their
attention on eternity, always go beyond the present existing
world. By alternating intimidation with flattery, the rulers
do their best to make these men their friends or to win them
over to their cause. Regimes of the most varied type surround
themselves with men of letters, or, as they are now called,
" intellectuals." As long as these " intellectuals " remain sub-
missive and offer themselves to the service of the State, to coin
theories or poems useful to the State, they cannot be anything but literary men and intellectuals of a poor quality, as
is to be expected. For those of a better type and of a finer
temperament, for the unruly ones, for the tormentors and
disturbers of themselves and of others, for the tempters and
seducers of souls, the poet of poets has put on the lips of the
politician the saying: " He thinks too much: such men are
dangerous "; and a theorist uttered the saying: " *Omnis
philosophia, cum ad communem hominum cogitandi facul-
tatem revocet, ab optimatibus non iniuria sibi existimatur
perniciosa.*"

But the moral life embraces both those who govern and their adversaries, conservatives and revolutionaries, and the latter perhaps more than the former, because better than the others they open the ways of the future and bring about the advancement of human society. For the moral life none are to be condemned except those who have not raised themselves to the moral life ; and it frequently praises, admires, loves and exalts those who are cast out by governments—the condemned and the vanquished—and sanctifies them as martyrs to an idea. For the moral life, every man of good will serves the cause of culture and of progress in his own way, all in a discordant harmony.

When " morality " has been conceived as the " ethical State " and the latter has been identified with the political State, or simply with the " State," we arrive at the concept —to which the theorists of that school do not demur—that concrete morality lies wholly in those who rule, in the act of their governing ; and their adversaries must be considered the adversaries of morality in action, deserving not only to be punished, with or without the sanction of the law, but also deserving the highest moral condemnation. This is, so to speak, a " governmental " concept of morality, the first appearance of which had a certain justification. This was in connection with the polemic against the romantic inclinations, the vagueness and presumtuousness of beautiful and sensitive souls, to which Hegel felt himself driven. Hence he thought it opportune to praise the good citizen over and above the man of genius and the hero. And even if this conception cannot be justified, it can, after all, be explained by Hegel's personal conservatism and by his loyalty to the Prussian State of the restoration. But we cannot understand how it can still be the object of such great fervour as is felt by the writers of the school, who seem to become inebriated and fall into ecstasy before the sublime image of the State. In spite of these exaltations and this Dionysiacal delirium over the State or government, we must insist that the State be considered what it really is : an elementary and narrow form of practical life, from every part of which the moral life issues and overflows, spreading out in abundant, productive streams ; so productive as to make and remake perpetually political life itself and States, that is, to compel them to renew themselves in conformity with the needs which political life creates.

III. POLITICAL PARTIES

THE problem of understanding the State and morality is a theoretical one and it belongs to the theorist. But the problem of " what to do ? " is a practical one, of the practical man, and, consequently, of the political man and of the ethico-political man. And yet it is so easy for this practical problem to fall into the error of a merely theoretical treatment, that it is well to insist on a matter which might seem obvious, namely, that the problem of behaviour does not consist in research and a philosophical statement, but in a deliberation and an act of the will. Apparently the responsibility for this action is so serious, and the perplexity of the deliberation so anguishing, that time after time an escape from that practical struggle is sought in theory and science, with the hope that these will provide the sure paths of action and will tell us with their solemn authority, " what to do." Certainly, one can argue about how to prevent revolutions and how to hold peoples in check, or, on the contrary, how to arouse and unleash them, how to overthrow existing governments. And, time and space being specified, one can argue as to the arrangement to be made of the modern world, of Europe, of Italy, or of one part or another of the Italian government and administration. But although these arguments assume the form of conclusions and exhortations, they are not solutions to practical problems, but methodical collections of data, their arrangement in series, the establishment of abstract relations between these abstract series, and the statement of the relation between causes. From the practical life they are divided as by a bottomless abyss. After all, who will put those plans into effect? And by that very act will not he who has put them into effect have modified them, adapted them to himself, and produced them anew, that is to say, asserted his own will? Not that these theoretical debates are entirely useless: they have the usefulness, common to all knowledge, of imparting information, and in some way they lend their colour to action. But indirectly, that is, because of the usual confusion as to what they really are, they help foster the erroneous idea that the means of achieving any desired end ought to be ascertained by the study of the end itself. It is not uncommon to hear the wistful proposal that we entrust to an international assembly of scientists the task of outlining, on the basis of Science, a programme or hygienic regime for humanity, which has suffered so many hardships throughout the centuries and is to-day still in suspense and deeply afflicted!

No, this is not the course to be followed. The political problem as a practical problem is a problem of enterprise, invention and creation, and therefore wholly individual and personal. All knowledge helps; but no single knowledge will ever tell me what I must do, because this is solely the secret of my own being and the discovery of my will. As long as the problem is stated in the impersonal and objective form: "What must the world do? What must Italy do?", it is stated in a form that is debatable in the abstract but insoluble in practice. What the world must and will do is known and will be known by the world and not by me; what Italy must and will do is known and will be known by Italy and not by me. On the contrary, the correct way of expressing the problem is: " What must I do?—I who live in the world, in Italy, etc."

The problem is always stated in this form and solved in the economic sphere, where each man seeks what is to his advan‧ tage or to his liking or to his taste and not to the liking of Italy, Europe or the world. So it is, too, in the political sphere, in so far as it is merely a political or utilitarian relation to which each man adapts himself as best he can, and from which he derives the greatest possible profit; or, when it is impossible for him to adapt himself to it, he tries to change it, in good ways and bad. Nor can this problem be stated and solved in another way in the ethical sphere, where it is a question of attaining a thing that goes beyond the individual, of putting into practice the universal and the good, but where this attainment is always the task of the individual, of one man, of a person, and must therefore be his own work, the work of individuality and personality at the service of the universal, universally conforming with and different from the work of every other individual. The belief that it is up to the individual who acts according to the moral code to do what the intellect ascertains and shows to be the good, that is historically attainable under the given circumstances, again changes the practical problem to a theoretical one, and, what is more, to an insoluble theoretical problem. The good of which we speak, an historically attainable good, is the dialectic product of the concordant discord of moral individuals, and will therefore, but cannot at present, be known by the individual who joins in the mystery of creation, just as the father does not know the son in whose creation he shares.

It is not to be feared that by this rejection of every ethical

intellectualism free rein is given to caprice, to pleasure and to
the whims of individuals, because the moral conscience
requires that each man, upon resolving to act, descends to the
depth of his own being and, with purity and humility of heart,
asks questions of and listens to the voice which speaks to him
and commands him; and it requires that he then follow with
resolute and courageous spirit his own " inner voice," whatever it may be, trusting in the Providence that directs human
affairs. Those various " inner voices " are nothing but the
needs of history personified in individuals and they gradually
assume their proper order in the maze, in the intricacy, in the
struggle of individual actions, gradually being translated into
actuality in the manner and degree possible to them. Thus,
when individuals decide, in the midst of conflicting reality and
of the infinite choices of action, they decide well when they
know they cannot do otherwise and must obey their *lex
singularis*. Consequently, in the general course of their lives
or in some aspects of it, they assert themselves as conservatives
or revolutionaries, authoritarians or liberals, aristocrats or
democrats, observers of tradition or breakers of tradition; by
thus defining themselves, they differentiate themselves from
others and at the same time with certain common and generic
names they draw near to others. Man's brief life seldom
permits versatility in the work that he accomplishes and in
the function that he discharges and therefore the " inner
voices," considered in their fundamental quality and character, are not ordinarily numerous in each individual. Therefore, although we do not deny that there are exceptions and
extraordinary cases, great credit is given in political life to
those who in the course of their public life play only one role,
as a guarantee that they have seriously searched and inquired
within themselves. On the contrary, there is a distrust of
changes and conversions, which, though they may sometimes

be corrections of a previous error or may have become necessary because of profound and unforeseen historical changes,
most frequently are signs of fickleness or of utilitarian interests
prevailing over ethical interests.

Unions between individuals who feel that they have more
or less similar needs and tendencies give rise, in the economic-
political sphere, to what are called " associations," " corporations " or " syndicates " and, in the ethico-political sphere, to
what are called " political parties," often likened to and confused, incorrectly, with economic groups. Common opinion,
or common thought (and regretfully, we must add, even
some philosophers, like Rosmini), fosters a great deal of ill-
feeling against parties. Why make divisions? they ask. If
we are divided on questions of public interest, it is a sign that
personal interests enter into them; otherwise, we would all be
in agreement. And the dream always dreamed by those who
reason thus is the dream of the one great political party, the
party with no other defect than that of being neither a party
nor political. But in our opinion, on the basis of what has
been said above, parties might be charged with the opposite
fault, that of weakening the energy of individual variations
and of reducing persons to flocks, held together by certain
common and generic tendencies, if they were actually to
carry out what is necessarily contained in their slogan of
uniformity and discipline. In reality, they do not carry it out,
and the parties are means offered to the various personalities
so that they may fashion for themselves instruments of action,
or so that they may assert themselves and, with themselves,
their own ethical ideals, and so that they may make efforts
to accomplish them. This accounts for the importance in the
parties of heads and leaders and also of the others who seem
to have positions of secondary importance and modestly withdraw to the shadows, yet manipulate the wires of action. The

important thing, then, is the vigour of the personality, in whom the ethical ideal is embodied and expressed; it is usually admitted that political parties have the character of the individuals who form and represent them.

Just as party discipline is nothing but the means by which political personalities succeed in holding their followers in their power for the actions to be performed, so each party develops an ideology or theory, or rather a pseudo-theory, which is useful for no other purpose than to create the appearance that it has as allies Truth, Reason, Philosophy, Science and History, deities which supposedly have deserted the camp of the adversary. But Philosophy and Science, and the other deities just mentioned, are impartial to all parties; or, better, they favour no party, since they are intent not on helping one party against the other, but on embracing and understanding them all. Taken by themselves, the pseudo-theories by which parties formulate their programmes may be correct and real, as, for example, the theory of historical development by antinomies, a theory with which liberalism with its progressiveness is connected. But the pseudo-theories have no connection with the party as political will, a will historically determined and individualized, the sole reason for which lies in itself (*stat pro ratione voluntas*); and in that forced relationship they become imbued with falsity. But in other cases, taken by themselves, the pseudo-theories are false as, for example, those Marxian theories on the surplus value and historical materialism and on the leap from the realm of necessity to that of liberty. At best, they express, in a form that is apparently logical but is intrinsically fanciful, the sentiments and the practical tendencies of the party. Nevertheless, even in these cases they fulfil their function. The ideologies have no function other than that of being the mouthpiece and defender of the party and sometimes exert their influence on the very members of the party and even on the leaders, making them prisoners in the nets of their own sophisms.

The "programmes," too, usually have a fictitious part, strategically valuable, representing the hopes and promises by which one party tries to win over the minds of men and emerge victorious in competition. But they have another part that is real, that which announces the intentions and proposals of the party. It is indispensable in order to give to the action a certain beginning and the general direction. This general direction cannot help being "indefinite" and therefore continually modified or denied in the succeeding action. The fictitious part of the programmes, their indefinite and ineffectual character, and the calculated or impulsive sophisms of the ideologies provide an opportunity, according to the common estimate, for a further and different criticism of parties : it is said that they exhibit nothing but lies and idle talk and that they lack all profundity. But it is clearly a superficial judgment which attacks ideologies and abstract programmes, but does not understand their instrumental function and therefore does not see that the substance and reality do not lie in such programmes, but in the actual wills of persons joined in those unstable organic and living associations which are called parties.

Since the moment at which the programmes most clearly reveal their abstract nature is not when they are wielded as offensive arms, but when they are put to the test, and above all when the parties come to power, a sharp line is usually drawn between being a partisan and governing; between a member of the party and a member of the government, or that same person risen to power; between the moment of criticism and of struggle, and the moment of doing and achieving. However, this difference, too, is merely empirical : social

c

life is completely a matter of reciprocal relationship and
responsiveness, and he who raises oppositions, criticizes and
questions, governs or, what amounts to the same thing, has
influence in the government; in the same way, he who
governs is a partisan; that is, he follows the impulse of the
party in which he is enrolled or of his own personality, which
is in itself a party. In this case, too, it would be foolish to
expect the individual to do what as an individual he cannot
do, because it is the work of Providence, work which lies
beyond the individual. And it would be foolish to expect
the individual to do the impossible by merely transferring
from one social position to another or from one place of work
or combat to another. The antitheses of parties find their
synthesis not in the government, but in history.

And history is the field in which one really finds differences
between political parties, that is, among individuals in their
various changeable groupings, which are not expressed and
differentiated, as is imagined, by the various " labels " with
which they are tagged. If the designations of parties were
drawn only from contingent and extrinsic facts, they would
have the advantage of referring the man in quest of information to the historical knowledge of the reasons and circumstances in which they were formed, just as the names of
people send us back to the direct observation and knowledge
of the real persons. But since the parties, as a result of their
ideologies and of the attempt to appropriate political theories
and fit them to their own, are frequently designated according
to the various phases of political theory, and separate the
inseparable and are called " liberal," " authoritarian,"
" democratic," " aristocratic," " monarchical," " socialist,"
etc., it is always easy for the sophistry of political passions to
change one designation to another, and to show that the true
liberal is the authoritarian, the true democrat the aristocrat,

the true socialist the antisocialist, the true republican the monarchist—a demonstration whose only disadvantage is that it can, with the same logic, be turned by the adversary to his own favour. But when names are treated as names and respected as such, and when in parties one seeks and contemplates their historical existence and the individuals who belong to them and guide them, these tricks of reciprocal transformation, these sophisms, are hindered or made useless. This is because in such cases we have before us the reality of the various parties, which is a diversity of sentiments, of temperaments, of precedences, of mental development, of culture, of education, of vocation. And it is then as impossible to confuse liberalism, authoritarianism and socialism as it is to mistake for each other the noble Piedmontese Camillo di Cavour, modernized in culture and in spirit, the Prussian *Junker* Otto von Bismarck, and the apocalyptic Jew, armed with Hegelian historical notions, Karl Marx.

IV. The Empirical Science of Politics

To those who are apparently dominated and overwhelmed by the spectacle of the States, of disputes and of political struggles, the philosophical propositions which we have been expounding will perhaps seem an extreme abstraction, almost a departure from the world for the region of the non-existent. But since these propositions, like all philosophical propositions, lead back to the creative spirit which is the sole and central source of everything, they are, instead, to the greatest degree concrete; whereas that materially conceived world, by which others allow themselves to be dominated and oppressed, is an abstract and untrue world. In those propositions all history is included, the past and the present (as Machiavelli would have said, " the experience of modern things and the lesson of ancient things "); and they are not understood well without the history to which they make references and illusions, just as history is not understood without them, for they are its soul. The aim of the philosophy of politics is to make clear the history of practical human activity, in its twofold form—as economic and merely political history and as ethico-political or moral history. This is not an aim which the philosophy of history looks forward to carrying out in the future, but one which it has always carried out; because history has always been thought about, in the form of narration and reflection, and for this reason there has always been philosophizing on politics and on morality, and there has always been a consciousness of what they really are. This consciousness has been more or less complex, coherent and systematic.

A legitimate need arises in the process of this knowledge, of fixing in mind what is known or that part of it which it is most urgent to remember, in the form which will make it easiest for the spirit to remember and have available. This is a legitimate need both for the necessities of action and as an aid for further research and new knowledge. This is the invariable origin, in every field of knowledge and action, of what is called " empirical science "; in our case, of the empirical science of politics.

This empirical science is reached through the reduction (to types and classes) of the innumerable facts of history, here chiefly economic or political history and ethico-political history. Facts are taken in the abstract content which is their matter, and deprived of their proper life, given by their spiritual form or individuality. The so-called empirical laws are based on classification, because to determine the characteristics of the various types of facts is the same as to organize these characteristics according to some system and to establish agreements and disagreements, concordances and discordances of effects. And, inasmuch as in all this continual fabrication of classes and of laws, one proceeds by abstraction, that is, by dividing the indivisible, there is continual recurrence to artificial concepts.

Thus, in order to fix in the memory those individuals and those actions which have the greatest importance in political life and which by comparison make other individuals and facts, also of a political nature, seem negligible and as though non-existent, it is imagined that "sovereignty," that is, the State itself, is found in certain persons and not in others; and the sovereignty or State, whose only reality lies in the relation which it constitutes, is personified. This opens the way for other artifices which try to bring into evidence certain modes of historical life (for example, the Athenian life), and therefore differentiate them from other modes (for example, the Persian). In order to attain this goal they build the frameworks of democratic, monarchical and aristocratic States. Similarly, in order to understand the relations in a State, between the various parts of the social or moral life, between the constitutional forms and the working of agriculture or of industry or of commerce, between economy and war, between religion and government, between the State and nations or languages, etc., similar cases are collected and the types of the theocratic, agricultural, commercial, industrial, military, national, pluri-national State, are set up. In fact, the first fallacy, which precedes all those we have mentioned, is the fallacy of single States, each one closed off from the others; whereas, in the aspect we are now considering, history is always universal history, that is, reality shows only whole sets of the most varied relations among all the inhabitants of the earth (not excluding the relations which may be established in the future with the inhabitants of other planets!). Only by some arbitrary intervention can these relations be divided into a series of state, intrastate and interstate relations. Yet, without these artifices it would not be possible to constitute the bodies of national, international, public, private, civil, penal, commercial law, etc.

The formation of the type of the mixed State, the division of the three powers of the State, the determining of the various goals which the State does or can set up for itself, the antithesis and the harmony between the concept of the State and that of the individual, the distinction of State from government, the characteristic features of the various parties in which the political struggle takes place, and many other concepts of this sort might be cited as examples of the work of classification which the empirical Science of politics is carrying on. And if more conspicuous examples of its laws were desired, it would be enough to mention the law of the rotation of political forms, each of which, through its own degeneration, passes on to the following one. And there are those other laws which establish a relation of concomitance between agricultural economy and the feudal constitution, between commercial economy and democracy; or again, the laws about political liberty and its beneficent effectiveness in fostering life, and about the depressing effect of absolutism and despotism, and other similar laws.

All these classifying and directional categories, laws, questions and problems form, then, the subject matter of Political Science, a science which does not need to be invented, because it can point to classical books, still alive and instructive to-day, in Greek and Roman literature, chief among them the treatise of Aristotle; and to books in the literature of the Renaissance, especially the Italian Renaissance, chief among them *The Prince, The Discourses* and the other writings of Machiavelli; and to the efforts of English, French and German writers

of the eighteenth and nineteenth centuries, from Montesquieu
to Treitschke. In recent times so-called Sociology has
been added, as a companion or rival, to Politics, as it
was traditionally called. Sociology, in that small part of
it which is not altogether contemptible, must be considered
an attempt to expand the old science by the inclusion of the
types and laws of some forms of life which belong to political
life but had been neglected because they did not refer to
public law, to government, to war and to diplomatic negotiations, all of which were usually directly associated with the
idea of politics.

To those who know the cause and genesis of empirical
science in general, and of the empirical science of politics
and sociology in particular, no pronouncement sounds more
preposterous than that made by some of the supporters of this
discipline (recently repeated in a well-known *Treatise on
Sociology*, written in Italian). Namely that empirical science
leaves philosophy aside and is founded directly on facts,
divorced from all philosophical speculations. The facts on
which it is founded are, at best, those facts which histories,
critically elaborated, hand down and explain; or, at worst,
they are the facts taken from the newspapers, histories of little
critical value which give information on the facts of yesterday
and to-day (newspapers are widely used in the above-
mentioned *Treatise*). And these histories and newspapers are
never anything but creations of the mind which thought—
that is, philosophy—produces by interpreting, and shaping
and qualifying actions and events. By giving a mere outline
of those accounts of facts and of those philosophical inter-
pretations empirical science has the power to deprive them of
soul and of meaning. But it cannot put them aside, and
therefore it cannot put aside the philosophy which has given
them life, any more than the butcher can do without the live

animals which he slaughters. Even in this case the dislike
expressed for philosophy serves only to prepare for the stealthy
introduction of a common or very poor philosophy and to
permit an outlet for passions and whims, lurking among the
severe theorems of the mechanical science which has made
the State and society its objects.

But, on the other hand, those who bear in mind the cause
and the genesis of the empirical science of politics understand
its function and necessity; and whereas they guard against
denying in its name the work of philosophy and of history
or against usurping their roles, they are careful to defend the
usefulness of that science against philosophical reasoners.
This is the usefulness defined by its own genesis, its usefulness
as an instrument. In this respect it would be pedantic, from
the philosophical point of view, to criticize the theory of
sovereignty, of the three forms of the State and of the three
powers, of the rotation of forms, of the purpose of the State,
of the rights of the citizen toward the State, of the distinction
between State and government, and all the other theories.
This criticism ceases to be pedantic and becomes valuable only
as a defence against the plans of the empirical science of
politics, when these plans, disguised as philosophical aphorisms
and taken as absolute principles, are transferred to philosophy
and history. Then philosophy and history rise in protest—
philosophy, which, through the empirical science of politics,
has witnessed the splitting of a unity, the separation of the
inseparable and everywhere the multiplication of artificial
concepts; and history, which in the same way has seen its
manifold varieties become uniform and its vivid and various
colours fade and merge. They protest because they had
willingly adapted themselves to these pauses in their work for
the advantage which might later come to the work itself; but
they cannot accept having what was to be an expedient for

their use changed to an obstacle. It is well that for certain purposes a distinction be made between monarchy and democracy; but this empirical distinction should not prevent our seeing that two monarchical States can have far more differences between themselves than exist between a monarchy and a democracy, because what matters from the historical point of view are not abstract forms, but concrete political and moral reality. It is well to try to combine differing forms with the hope of avoiding certain disadvantages and attaining what used to be known as the "mixed State" or the "excellent State"; but it must not be forgotten that only the State which seeks to promote the advancement of mankind, whatever may be the class or classes in which the abstract form of its constitution may later be placed, is an excellent State; nor must it be forgotten that in the final analysis States are what the men who constitute them continually make them, with their mind and with their spirit, which alone lend meaning and give life to forms of government. There is pedantry in political science just as there is pedantry in literary science. Neither the wisdom of antiquity, nor the Renaissance with its subtle reasoning and combination of forms, nor the modern era, the era of the constitutions, escaped this pedantry. The fundamental question is always: "Who undertakes all these things?" A poet, a philosopher, a saint, a simple and resolute man are worth more in political reality than all the political theorists and are able to do what the latter cannot do. And it is well that we should define parties empirically as the liberal, the conservative, the radical or the socialist. However, the real problem is not how to be a good liberal, a good conservative, a good socialist or a good radical, but how to act in certain given circumstances in a manner suitable to reality, which is neither radical nor socialist nor conservative nor liberal. It is well, finally, to devise new institutions to

settle arguments between the various States; but it must not
be imagined that thereby there has been or will be first
brought into being the Society of peoples, the unity of mankind or the World State, because this society, this unity, this
World State has always existed and is called history. The
life of this *civitas mundi* flows and will flow at times in a
peaceful manner, at times in a troubled and violent manner,
exactly like the life of the single *civitates* or States.

The laws of the empirical science of politics, when presented
as maxims and advice, have the same auxiliary function, and
not the function of a determining force, toward the decision
of the will. Are maxims and advice useless? It is customary
to say that advice is offered with the consciousness that
it will not be followed. This is true. But it should be
added that advice is not offered in order to be followed, but
is given as advice, as practical possibilities offered to those
who are experiencing difficulty in reaching a decision, so that
they may not overlook these possibilities in searching for the
solution they are about to reach. Even if this advice is not
accepted, it will nevertheless be weighed mentally and with
some effect on the decision. Or, if this advice is followed,
the case is certainly no different, because the decision and the
action are identical with the advice only in appearance, and
in reality differ from it in so far as they are the decision and
the action of the individual, created by the individual. Going
still further, it might even be said that advice is offered in
order not to be followed. The conclusion expressed or understood in every honest advice is: " See for yourself." That
demagogue, Spedito of Porta San Piero, of whom Villani
speaks, was not entirely wrong. Villani tells us that, with
his ardent words, he incited the Florentines to the battle which
ended in the defeat at Montaperti. After the disaster, the
demagogue, now in exile, was reprimanded by one of his

opponents, Tegghiaio Aldobrandi, of Dantean memory, for having brought the Florentines and himself to so much misery by his advice. He boldly answered, "And why did you believe in it?" Actually, he was merely practising his profession, in conformity with his character. The profession of demagogue was one which Providence had assigned to him, a profession useful as a stimulus and as a catalyst. And the others, the thoughtful and sensible ones, indifferent to the favour of the populace, should have practised their profession better than they did, should have resisted more strongly until victory was theirs, and should not have succumbed to the oratory of the demagogue; then they would not have had to share the responsibility for what had happened.

Why have I insisted on pointing out, with the greatest care, the distinction between theory and practice, between the philosophy of politics and politics? To urge the philosophers to be modest and not to confuse political life, already sufficiently confused, with inopportune and feebly argued philosophy? Yes, of course. I had that idea too. But I confess that I was moved, above all, by the opposite desire, namely, to save historical judgment from contamination with practical politics, a contamination which deprives historical judgment of tolerance and fairness. This desire is also, in its own way, politics, profound politics, if what Aristotle, the father of political science, used to say is true, about the contrast between the active and the contemplative life—that not only the actions which turn towards the facts are practical, but even more practical are the contemplations and reflections which have their origin and end in themselves and which, by educating the mind, prepare for good deeds.

Chapter II

CONCERNING THE HISTORY OF THE PHILOSOPHY OF POLITICS

I. MACHIAVELLI AND VICO. POLITICS AND ETHICS

THE name of Machiavelli has become almost the symbol of pure politics and it certainly marks a sharp crisis in the development of the science. Not that antiquity did not have some inkling of the distinction and contrast between politics and ethics: this is shown in the very fact that their subject matter was attributed to two different disciplines; and debates like those on just and unjust law, on natural and conventional law, on force and justice, etc., show how the contrast was sometimes felt and how the correlative problem appeared in outline. But the contrast never came to the forefront and never became the focus of deep study and meditation. This did not even happen in the long centuries of the domination of Christian thought, because the contrast between the *civitas Dei* and the *civitas terrena,* and later between Church and Empire, had its solution in the doctrine of the double rule instituted by God, or possibly in the doctrine of the supremacy of Church over Empire or of Empire over Church; and it was not sharpened by philosophical dissension. But there is no doubt that Christian thought, in which the examination of the moral consciousness plays so great a part, was preparing, by making this consciousness more keen, the dissension that was to break out. Niccolò Machiavelli is considered a pure expression of the Italian Renaissance; but he should also be connected in some way with the movement of the Reformation, with that general need, which asserted itself in his time, in

44

Italy and elsewhere, to know man and to study the problem of the soul.

It is known that Machiavelli discovered the necessity and autonomy of politics, of politics which is beyond or, rather, below moral good and evil, which has its own laws against which it is useless to rebel, politics that cannot be exorcized and driven from the world with holy water. This is the concept which pervades all his works. Although this concept is not formulated with that didactic and scholastic exactness which is usually mistaken for philosophy, and although it is sometimes disturbed by fantastic idols, by figures that waver between political virtue and wicked lust of power, it must nevertheless be termed a profoundly philosophical concept, and it represents the true foundation of a philosophy of politics.

But what usually passes unobserved is the decided bitterness with which Machiavelli accompanies this assertion of politics as an intrinsic necessity. " If all men were good," he says, these precepts " would not be good." But men are " ungrateful and fickle; they flee from dangers and are eager for gains." Therefore it is well to see to it that you are feared rather than loved, to provide first for fear and then, if possible, for love. You must learn " to be not good." You must fail to keep your word when it is to your advantage to do so, because otherwise others would fail to keep their word to you; you must defeat those who are waiting for the opportunity to defeat you. Machiavelli yearns for an unattainable society of good and pure men; and he fancies it is to be found in the distant past. In the meantime he prefers the less civilized peoples to the more civilized, the people of Germany and the mountaineers of Switzerland to the Italians, the French and the Spanish (then at the height of their glory), who are the " corruption of the world." It is his feeling, and he expresses it with a shudder, that whoever reads of the horrors which history relates to us " will undoubtedly, if he is born of man, be frightened by every imitation of the evil times and will be kindled by the great desire to follow the good times." In the face of such evident signs of a stern and sorrowful moral conscience, it is amazing that there has been so much idle talk about Machiavelli's immorality; but the common people term as moral only moralistic unctuosity and bigoted hypocrisy. The lack of this bitter pessimism distinguishes Guicciardini from Machiavelli. The former feels only a sort of contempt toward men in whom he finds so " little goodness," and he settles down peacefully in this discredited world, aiming only at the advantage of his own " personal being." If he had not had to serve the Medici popes because of this " personal being " of his, he would have loved " Martin Luther more than himself," because he would have hoped that the rebel friar might undo the ecclesiastic state and destroy the " wicked tyranny of the priests." Guicciardini's man is different in temperament from Machiavelli's man.

It is still more important to observe that Machiavelli is as though divided in spirit and mind with respect to the politics whose autonomy he has discovered. At times it seems to him a sad necessity to have to soil his hands by dealing with ugly people, and at times it seems to him a sublime art to found and support that great institution which is the State. Quite often he speaks of the State in a religious tone, as when he recalls the saying that one must be prepared for the sake of the State to lose not only one's reputation, but also the salvation of one's own soul; or as when he looks back, with ill-concealed envy, at the pagan religion, which exalted, as the highest good, honour in this world, extolling human glory, and praising greatness of spirit, strength of body, and all the virtues which make man powerful; whereas the Christian religion, by showing the truth and the real way to the world beyond, despises this world, and praises abjection, setting contemplative men above the others, and endurance above action. Is politics diabolical or divine? Machiavelli imagines it in the guise of the Centaur, described by poets as a very beautiful creature, part man part beast, and he describes his prince as half man and half beast. In order that there may be no doubt as to the integrity of the human self of this creature, he assigns even the subtleties of the mind, such as craftiness, to the animal self, recommending that it be part fox and part lion, because the lion does not defend himself against traps and the fox does not defend himself against wolves. One would be acting as a novice in the art of ruling if one wished " always to carry on as a lion." The art and science of politics, of pure politics, brought to maturity by the Italians, were to him a source of pride. For this reason he answered Cardinal de Rohan, who used to tell him that the Italians knew nothing about war, by saying that " the French knew nothing about the State."

The continuation of Machiavelli's thought must not be sought among the Machiavellians, who continue his political casuistry and body of maxims and write about the " raison d'état," frequently mixing moralizing trivialities with these maxims : nor among the anti-Machiavellians, who proclaim the fusion and identification of politics with morality and conceive States founded on pure dictates of goodness and justice : nor among the eclectics, who place in juxtaposition theories of morality and theories of politics, and take the edge off antinomies and make them empirical, instead of solving them, and change them to misfortunes and inconveniences which happen in life but have the character of accidental things. It must be sought in those who made an effort to classify the concept of " prudence," of " shrewdness " and, in short, of " political virtue," without confusing it with the concept of "moral virtue" and, also, without in the least denying the latter. (One of these was Zuccolo, a seventeenth century writer.) And it must be sought in some powerful spirits who, beyond the shrewdness and sagacity of the individual, as analyzed by Machiavelli, asserted the divine work of Providence. Such a person was Tommaso Campanella.[1] But Machiavelli's true and worthy successor, the powerful intellect who gathered together and strengthened both these scattered suggestions of criticisms and the immortal thought of the Florentine secretary, was another Italian, Vico. In truth, the whole philosophy of politics in its central idea is symbolized in two Italians. Vico is not kind to Machiavelli, yet is full of his spirit which he tries to clarify and purify by integrating Machiavelli's concept of politics and of history, by settling his theoretical difficulties and by brightening his pessimism.

For Vico, politics, force, the creative energy of States, becomes a phase of the human spirit and of the life of society, an eternal phase, the phase of certainty, which is followed eternally, through dialectic development, by the phase of truth, of reason fully explained, of justice and of morality, or ethics. The symbol of the Centaur now appears inadequate : what once seemed to be the animal part of man is found to be a human part too, the first form of the will and of action, the premise of all others. Humanity does not spring forth without passion, without force, without authority. Strong men are the best, and from the harsh rule of strong men come the civilized and refined societies which form a contrast to that rule and which, nevertheless, would not exist without that generous barbarity. And from time to time they must renew this strength by reverting to that barbarity. So

---

[1] Cf. for the period from Machiavelli to Vico the treatment of the Italian political theorists of the seventeenth century in Croce, *Storia dell' età barocca in Italia*, Bari, Laterza, 1929, Part I, Chapter II ; cf. also Chapter VI.

Machiavelli used to say that the States must from time to time be called back to their principles, thus generalizing the maxim, professed by Florentine partisans, that every five years it was fitting " to seize again the State," that is " to cause men the same terror and fear which they had caused in seizing the State." Thus, if Machiavelli becomes religious in dealing with the art of the State, Vico does not hesitate to speak of the " divinity of force." Like Machiavelli, who used to find " the mountaineers in whom there is no civilization " more pliant to the touch of the politician's hand—because " a sculptor will more easily make a beautiful statue from a rough piece of marble than from a piece badly roughhewn by others,"—Vico, too, approved of a more vigorous vitality in the barbarous peoples, thanks to which they are better able to create new States. On the other hand, still according to Vico, civilized and corrupt peoples cannot be reformed; statues that are badly cast and spoiled must be thrown into the furnace and smelted all over again. Brutality and treachery, unavoidable in politics and recognized and recommended by Machiavelli, even though he, felt a moral disgust for them, are explained by Vico as a part of the drama of humanity, which is in a perpetual state of creation and recreation. They are viewed in their double aspect of real good and apparent evil, that is, good that takes on the appearance of evil for the sake of the higher good, which indeed springs up from its very heart. In this way bitterness is replaced by the consideration of rational necessity and by the feeling of trust in Providence, which governs human affairs.

Such is the unconscious similarity of Machiavelli to Vico and the involuntary Machiavellianism of Vico, not expressly formulated in their pages, but as we obtain it both from their scattered ideas, and from their judgments and biases, their likes and dislikes. It reveals itself to the expert eye of those

D

who have followed the development of thought and life after Machiavelli and Vico and who, therefore, understand those things at which Machiavelli and Vico aimed even better than they themselves could.

II. ROUSSEAU—NATURAL LAW

WHEN we turn from Machiavelli and Vico to the Social Contract we have the impression of no longer knowing in what world we are. Certainly we are not in the world of political history nor in the world of the philosophy of politics. Machiavelli's problem was that of asserting the real quality and the necessity of politics as politics; Vico's problem that of understanding how harsh and violent politics goes hand in hand with ethical life. But Rousseau's problem is not of this kind. Fundamentally, it is not a problem which refers to the study of·reality. As he himself says, with him it is a matter of seeking out a form of association, in which " each individual joins all others, yet obeys only himself and thus remains as free as before."

We can observe in everyday life this tendency with regard to reality, to seek the criterion for judgment and the model for action, not in reality itself, not, that is, in historical and spiritual reality, but in nature conceived above and beyond history, in reason conceived as pure reason, as an idea devoid of reality. Each one of us, especially in his youthful years, has had this impulse, even though fleetingly. Since nature apart from history and reason without reality are abstractions, those who thus state the problem of judging and acting are called abstract intellects. And as abstraction from reality, pure reason, is nothing more than the mathematical attitude of the human spirit, their constructions are called geometrical or mechanical; and it is a mistake to use these constructions as a foundation, which is what we do when we treat them as solid things or, even worse, as criteria for judgment and guides for action.

This tendency, which is continually reappearing in reflection and is experienced longer in certain periods of individual life, was predominant in that age of European history (about two centuries, extending from the end of the sixteenth to the end of the eighteenth) which derived from it its name of " the Age of Reason," or because of its closer conformity to the theory of politics, the age of natural law or rights. The problem, then, was no longer philosophical and historical, nor even precisely practical *de optimo statu,* but *de statu rationali,* in conformity with the reckoning, measuring and calculating reason, which starts out with equal or unequal quantities and, by combining them, sets them in a state of equilibrium. At the same time the mathematical science of nature was developing; and the mental habit which was forming in this science was being transferred to all fields, to philosophy, to history, to politics. It is characteristic that the new science concerning human activity which arose at that time should be precisely the science of utility made mathematical, political Arithmetic, as it was first called, or Economics, as we call it. Rousseau's book is an extreme form, or one of the extreme forms, and certainly the most famous, of the school of natural law.

This school undoubtedly had a great political importance in so far as it provided the innovators with arms and flags in those centuries during which the last vestiges of the Middle Ages and of feudal and clerical privileges were being hunted out of existence and modern society was established. It provided them with arms because the concept of plain nature and of abstract reason denied all the laborious and complicated product of history, and affirmed only reality, rational reality, to be made and remade with the aid of right reason. In the name of that concept it was possible to discredit and clear away all existing institutions, laws and customs, which, since they were ill tolerated, odious or troublesome, were at that time disdainfully termed gothic or barbarian, products of the sad era of fanaticism and superstition. And this school provided flags, that is, resplendent symbols, by building mechanical models of society which had no life by themselves but received life from the impulses, the desires, the hopes of the innovators. Thus, the most widely varied political programmes were clothed with the same mathematical and mechanical form—from the programme of the absolutists, who intended to strengthen the monarchy against the clergy and the nobility and did not doubt that the monarchy was based on divine right, to the programme of the democrats and quasi-communists, who proclaimed, as did Rousseau, the sovereignty of the people or the will of the nation.

But, however great the polemic effectiveness of those beliefs and of those constructions was and is (since we all see how much power the so-called democratic ideals still have to-day), however great this effectiveness may be in the future, it is certain that those constructions, understood as doctrines or criteria for the explanation of facts, were and are simply absurd, and they were presented as doctrines, at times as philosophical doctrines, aspiring to offer the true concept on which political judgments should be based: at times as historical doctrines, designating forms of society which had existed at one time or existed more or less completely in some place, and were sure to be attained in the future. It is natural that all those who retained a sense of political reality should protest against these fantastic and empty dreams; and that especially those who inherited the spirit of Machiavelli and of Vico should protest, by satire and mockery.

The foremost Machiavellian satirist of the eighteenth century was the abbot Galiani, a politician of the old Italian school who, at a certain moment in his life, chanced to fall among the naturalists, the economists, the encyclopædists and the abstractionists of Paris. He looked upon them with amazement, almost as though they were strange fanatics, and later buried them under a shower of gay critical witticisms and mockery. But Vico in person, and not through his disciples, had confronted the antipolitical and antihistorical school of natural law, as it had already been outlined in Grotius and in Pufendorf, and in the Cartesian philosophy, that is, the school at its beginning. Vico had foreseen in this school and in the superficial character of the knowledge and judgment which it induced, the end of every serious science, just as Galiani later caught a glimpse in it of the imminent Jacobinism and the Terror. And although other thinkers later took, spontaneously, the same position which Vico had taken and defended, it is nevertheless worthy of note that Joseph De Maistre, one of the first critics of political rationalism, had paid attention to Vico's *Scienza nuova* and that Cuoco, the first writer who arose in Italy against the rationalism of the French revolution, had studied both Vico and De Maistre. However, this criticism of naturalistic rationalism, which originated with Vico, the concept of law and politics as history, which succeeded it, prevailed in the following century with the coming of romanticism and philosophical idealism.

Philosophical idealism did not fail to render a deserved, though general, homage to rationalism and the enlightenment, both of which it had superseded. This it did because it recognized that even in the form of abstract and mathematical reason and of individualistic and atomic liberty, rationalism and the enlightenment had asserted reason, liberty and the new humanism against the old transcendentalism.

III. Hegel—The Ethical State

WHAT we have called political life and the State in the
narrow or true sense of the word corresponds more or less
to what Hegel called the " civil society " (bürgerliche Gesell-
schaft). It included not only the economic activity of men,
the production and exchange of goods and services, but also
the law and administration or government by laws. It was
not, therefore, without reason that later on Marx, starting
with this concept, considered the juridical and political order
a simple " superstructure " of an economic character, as it
actually is. This partial truth led him into the error of
considering even morality and all the rest a superstructure.
But Hegel did not realize that the State, understood in the
narrow sense, is precisely the formation which he had
encountered and christened a mere " civil society." For this
reason he insisted on going higher than both family and civil
society in what he defined as " Ethics " or the " State." His
definition remained a hybrid and equivocal concept wavering
between the universal aspect of the moral spirit and the
specific character of the political spirit. This can be seen in
several places, as for instance, where Hegel endeavours to
solve the conflict between politics and morality.[2] He feels
that such a problem rises from a weakness of concepts and
he sets it aside with contempt; but he is certainly far from
a logical solution of the problem and he can only bring
against it the argument that " the welfare (das Wohl) of a
State justifies actions which would not be justified by the
welfare of an individual." This is a point calling for proof
because, since the individual State is considered here as an
individual existence, it is not clear why it should have a right
which is denied to the individual. It certainly does not have
that right because it represents several or many individuals.

---

[2] Cf. Hegel, *Philosophie des Rechts.*

This would be an arithmetical, not an ethical difference. The one case can only be differentiated from the other by saying that the State functions according to an ethical principle; whereupon we reach the following dilemma: either to deny the individual State by giving value to the ethical spirit alone, or to deny the ethical spirit by holding out before it the recalcitrant individual States.

But does Hegel really preserve here the individual States, which are abstractions? People have failed to observe that Hegel, by having the first phase of the State, internal law, followed by the second phase, foreign law, does not admit any possibility of unification in this second phase. Rather, Hegel refutes and almost mocks at the Kantian idea of perpetual peace, and sees war as the only solution to arguments between individual States. As the final phase, as the synthesis which surpasses the thesis of internal law and the antithesis of foreign law, he places History. He says: " In the reciprocal relation between States, inasmuch as they behave as individual States, there develops on a large scale the rather exciting game of the internal individuality of passions, of interests, of aims, of talents and virtues, of violence, of injustice and of vices; and that of exterior fortuitousness, a game in which the very body of ethics, the independence of the State, is exposed. The principles of the national spirits are all limited because of their peculiarities, in which, as living individuals, they have their objective reality and their self-consciousness. Their destinies and acts in their reciprocal relation are the dialectics of the finitude of these spirits, from which the universal spirit, the spirit of the world, arises unlimited and has its being; and, as a universal tribunal, it exercises its supreme right on them in the history of the world."

This means that real morality or ethics is not put into action in the individual State, but in the struggle, peace and renewed struggle between the individual States, in which each individual fulfils his duties and every moral man is moral, whatever the State of which he is a member and servant. Having recognized the struggle between individual States in the so-called external right, one cannot help recognizing it within each State, in the so-called internal right, as a struggle between parties which compete with each other and succeed one another in governments, etc. Indeed, the distinction between individual States can no longer be maintained firmly in history, except in an empirical manner and for purposes of convenient representation and discourse. Even within the States individuals are moral or immoral, not in so far as they obey or rebel against the government of the time, but in so far as they are such in their inner selves or in their conscience.

Hegel himself was unaware of this implicit denial which he made of his " ethical State," that is, of his " ethics as State " ; nor were his disciples aware of it, not even Spaventa.[3] This accounts for the present diffusion in Italy of an equivocal idolatry of the State.

Hegel the philosopher is to be distinguished from Hegel the writer and the politician. On this matter the followers of the theory of the ethical State are still confused to-day, for they identify the true and profound criticisms which Hegel raised against the abstract or atomistic individualism of Rousseau's political doctrine with his attitude toward the politics of his time and the ideals which he thought should be promoted for the future—an attitude which is neither true nor false, but his own. Hegel was convinced that the Protestant countries, like Prussia, having already completed their revolution with the Lutheran Reformation, should now enjoy peace; and he was convinced that revolutions con-

[3] Cf. Spaventa, *Principi di Etice,* Gentile ed., Naples, 1904.

cerned only the Catholic countries, which for this reason were the countries of liberalism.   He used to say, " With this formal liberty, with this abstraction, no strong organization can arise.   Liberty immediately opposes all the particular measures of the government, because they are the expression of a particular will and therefore arbitrary.   The will of the majority overthrows the ministry, and the party that had been the opposition takes over the government; but the government again has the many against it.   Thus, movement and restlessness continue.   This is the conflict, the Gordian knot, the problem which history now has before it, and which must be solved in the future." [4]

The century following Hegel solved the problem by showing that one not only lives with liberalism but thrives only on it.   Since Hegel included Italy among the disturbed and unhappy Catholic countries, and recalled the revolutions of 1820–21,[5] which, like the Spanish revolution, had been, as he put it, "merely political, with religious innovations," and consequently doomed to fail, as in fact they did, it may be remarked that liberalism itself became a religion in Italy, and when fused with the nationalistc sentiment produced something that proved to be more lasting than the imperialist, historically famous, monarchy of the Hohenzollerns.

This is a defeat not so much for Hegel the politician as for Hegel the philosopher, who was still tied to the concepts of a higher and perfect form of political life and of a final and ultimate state of history.   These are inconsistent with that historical outlook which, from another point of view, he planted so firmly in modern European culture.

[4] Cf. Hegel, *Philosophie der Geschichte*, Lasson's edition, pp. 943–33; cf. pp. 925–28.

[5] Even in this his sentiments were nothing but an echo of those of King Frederick William III, of the crown prince, of the Prussian absolutists and also of their zealous adviser, Metternich.

IV. The State According to Haller

HEGEL criticized Haller, the author of the *Restauration der Statswissenschaft,* in an unusually violent manner.   He accused him of having failed to recognize what is rational and infinite in the State and accused him therefore of being completely lacking in reasoning power.   Haller, like almost all the political theorists and like Hegel himself, actually introduced in his book a particular political tendency of his own. This was a bias toward the patriarchal State, of the medieval German type or, more specifically, of the Swiss type as found in Berne—a political ideal certainly more antiquated and narrower than that of the Prussian State of the Restoration, which Hegel favoured.   And it must be admitted also that he was not very profound or exact in philosophy.   But, even with these admissions, the judgment usually given of this writer (now almost completely forgotten) does not seem to me just. There is in his work a theoretically important implication, although it is in the part most bitterly criticized by Hegel and by other critics : it is the concept of the State as a relation of private law.   By relation of private law we mean that relation which is merely legal or which has a purely economic basis.   But later, if it suits our purpose, we shall either nullify as empirical the distinction between private and public law, making the two terms coincide (every law is both private and public); or we shall maintain this distinction, giving to the second term an ethical meaning (the truly public law, that is, the universal law, is no longer a mere law).   For Haller princes are neither the administrators of public affairs, nor the chief servants of the State, nor the higher officials or functionaries, nor simply the heads of the State ; but, on the contrary, they are entirely free persons, who in reality govern not the affairs of other men, but only their own.   Subjects do not exist for the prince or for his advantage alone, but they have reciprocal obligations with him, since each one seeks his own advantage in the service rendered and must consequently fulfil the duties connected with this service. Haller says: " According to the right, in conformity with the law of strict justice, each man exists for himself and constitutes the object of his own actions." He also says that the States are not complete and perfect associations between men, but relations of service, having no other aim and resulting in no further relationship.

This is a completely economic character which coincides with the character of the " civil society " as defined by Hegel and, like it, does not intend to comprise the whole of humanity, but merely a phase of it. In fact, Haller does not forget—as might be thought by those who base their judgment on Hegel's diatribe against him—that the relation that is dependent strictly on law or on private right is surpassed by the moral relation. He says: " They are two different problems: one, to know what authority is based on and how far it extends, and the other, to know how this authority must be exercised; it is one thing to say that the strongest is master, and another to say what use he must make of his strength." According to the juridical relation, each man exists for himself; but according to the moral relation, according to the law of charity, each man is created to help his fellow man.

Of course, the emphasis given by Haller to the " Princes," the " strong," the " sovereign," almost as though they were absolute positions, may not seem entirely accurate. Nor is it corrected by the modifications which the author introduces into it, by pointing out that the need to dominate is balanced by the need to be dominated; that the blessings of peace are realized only between unequal forces, whereas equal forces clash and have struggles; that subordination, being in conformity with nature, does not offend self-respect at all; that the strongest are everywhere the most generous, etc. According to Haller, even in the beginning, the people do not exist before the prince, but the prince before the people, just as the father before his children, the master before his servants, the root and the trunk before the branches and the leaves. He considers it the characteristic of the sovereign prince to be independent, and maintains that this characteristic is the only one which really distinguishes States from other associations and relations of interests.

But, on the other hand, when he undertakes to approach more closely this concept of independence, he can only say, vaguely, that "independence in itself often consists of a slightly higher degree of liberty, power, reputation and renown." And, going further, he makes a statement which is a criticism of his theory of sovereignty—that by this road men finally reach the " great truth that all those which we call States or civil societies are nothing more than an imperceptible and uninterrupted progression of unequal fortunes, an infinitely complicated number of reciprocal needs and particular conventions; that each man is naturally surrounded by inferiors, by superiors and by equals; that everyone rules over his inferiors, obeys the will of his superiors and shares a part of the rights with his equals; and, finally, that in the final analysis God alone is the master, and that we are all his people, since the strongest among us have received their sovereign power only from the supreme lord, from the Creator of nature who gives it and takes it away, who changes power and fortunes, and seats and unseats kingdoms." Just as Hegel's individual States found their conclusion in the " history of the world," analogously, and not very differently, Haller's States find their conclusion in God.

To the merit in Haller that we have already pointed out

must be added another, which Hegel himself recognizes to a certain extent, namely, his criticism of the atomistic theory of equality. For Haller, who does not admit governments of democracies, but only of aristocracies, the representative system itself is simply " another word to designate aristocracy in the midst of an association that is false or at least extended by an artifice." He dismisses the " state of nature," which played so great a part in the speculation of the two preceding centuries, by declaring that the social state is likewise " of nature," and that this state and the extrasocial state always exist, both at the same time; that is, the extrasocial state exists not only among princes, as was recognized by the theory of the right of war and peace attributed to them, but among all those who do not have particular reciprocal ties, contracts of service and of society, and stand before each other as one individual before another.

In general, the reactionary writers should be read for their strong feeling for the State as both authority and mutual consent, and as an institution which goes beyond the pleasure of abstract individuals, and also for their opposition to theories of equality as well as Jacobinism, since they were opposed not only to " geometrical governments," but to all governments founded *a priori* and without basis and historical continuity. Thus the Catholic Baader,[6] declares that authority is not " an inhibiter, but a giver of force " (*nicht ein Krafthemmendes, sondern ein Kraftgebendes*), and that submission never comes about as of one man to another man, but as of men, the so-called sovereign and the so-called subjects, to a third (authority), which is not a man, but a relation, a universal concept, which Baader identifies with the personal God. The defect of these writers lies in their lack of any dialectical comprehension of history, as well as in their

[6] Baader, *Grundzüge der Societätsphilosophie,* 2nd ed., Würzburg, 1865.

transcendental religious concept. For this reason they
attribute an eternal character to passing political forms and
they fail to see that even the antihistorical and anti-
philosophical theories of equality were of value as evidence
of a new generation and a new spirit, and of approaching
political developments, even if they had no value as theories.
They do not fully understand past history, because they sin
against the rights of the future.

V. ECLECTIC THEORIES

THE view we have supported as to the completely utilitarian
or economic quality of the State, or, more clearly, of political
action, is necessary in order to establish firmly the concept of
morality, which assimilates an individual action, making it
moral, and in the same manner assimilates the State. After
all, the State is really nothing but a great number of successive
actions. But it is a difficult concept and consequently it is not
possible to maintain it and draw all the conclusions which
flow from it without great effort. These difficulties exist in
the field of politics no less than in the fields of economics and
of law, all of which are part of one and the same field. The
eclectic position is an easier one; which through reflection on
common sayings arrives at the realization that politics is not
morality. A certain difference is admitted, but we strive to
temper and reconcile it and, in the long run, instead of
mediating between the two principles, as should be our duty,
we let them alternate or play hide and seek. In this
parallelism of morality and politics lies the danger that
practically the same thing will happen that Aristotle used to
say happened in weighing and parcelling out virtues and other
possessions leading to happiness (riches, money, power, reputation, etc.), namely that, with morality reduced to the status

of a good or of one duty among many, men will be content with a modest portion of virtue, whereas they will require limitless quantities of the other possessions.

Such eclecticism appears even in the worthiest treatises on politics, like Bluntschli's treatise and also Treitschke's treatise —the latter falsely reputed to be a theorist of pure force—or in Janet's well-known history of political sciences. Bluntschli says that the moralists ask for impossible things and that the political sophists ask for things which are harmful to morality. How are we to get out of this labrynth? He answers that we are to do so by thinking that the State is, of course, a moral entity, but that it is concerned with the order of external life common to men; and that therefore the moral exigencies experienced by politicians are governed by norms different from those which religion imposes on men. But we should no longer let ourselves be deluded by the words " internal " and " external," which are entirely without meaning in reality, because reality is not divided into an inner and outer part. Bluntschli goes on to say that private morality and political morality have the same basis in the universal ethical order, and are two trunks of the same root. Notwithstanding, " the instinct of peoples has set up a great difference between private and political morality," because, in effect, evil taken by itself, which the private individual is expected to avoid, is a different thing from evil seen as part of the whole, in which it is subordinate to good. This latter evil is permissible to the statesman, who keeps his eyes fixed on his goal. Therefore, as assimiliation is admissible in politics when it is not committed for base and personal motives, but for the lasting security and prosperity of society, and when it is necessary to that end. But we no longer allow ourselves to be deceived by the concept of what is permissible, a concept which should be relegated to the old casuistry of the Jesuits. Janet recognizes in words that " political philosophy is a science which has its own principles and its particular laws and which deals with any other order "; but at the same time he considers it " useful and even necessary not to separate it at all from moral philosophy, another science to which it is naturally bound by a thousand different ties." Moral philosophy would assign " the true purpose " to politics. This purpose, assigned to it by morality, would, of course, be moral, but limited. This purpose would be in no way " to contradict virtue," but " to protect the right," to exercise justice and not virtue. Limited to this function, the existence of politics is transitory or, at most, earthly; in this it differs from morality. Janet says that " the object of government is to prepare men imperceptibly for this perfect state of society, wherein laws and the government itself would become useless." Even Treitschke holds to the external theory and to the concept of law as external life; and he rejects the Hegelian ethical State because " the State is not the whole life of the people, but merely embraces this life as guardian and organizer." For him, too, the relation between politics and morality " is not very simple and clear," and he makes statements and contradicts them, and is horrified at the " profound immorality " of Machiavelli's political theory, but then does not recognize any limitations to the State's duty to preserve itself. He confesses that " there are, alas, in the life of the State, as in the lives of individuals, innumerable cases in which the use of entirely pure means is impossible." This same weakness is found again in Rümelin's famous introduction, *Über das Verhältnis der Politik zur Moral* (1874), in which the invectives against Machiavelli are renewed, but in which it is asserted that moral norms which are obligatory for the individual do not concern the State, which is itself the giver of norms. Fundamentally, Rümelin repeats Hegel's position, but makes it worse by changing it from a dialectical position to a classificatory and static one. In fact, for Rümelin politics and morals are two co-ordinated classes, both subordinate to Ethics, which is a higher class.

It may be that there are some who would be pleased with this seemingly scientific and philosophical thinking, which reproduces the uncertainty and immaturity of common thought. But we think it is useful to get rid of it, even at the risk of making an effort which at first takes on the aspect of an extreme and paradoxical assertion.

VI. THE HISTORY OF THE PHILOSOPHY OF POLITICS

THE foregoing remarks, in addition to clarifying historically some references made in the previous essay, are of value as showing in a practical way, with a few names of persons and with a few examples, how a "history of the Philosophy of politics" can be treated. This history is to be separated from two other histories with which it is usually incorrectly associated; the "history of political science," that is, the history of the empirical science of politics, of the classifications and of the laws gradually built up in this field of experience; and the "history of practical tendencies," that is, of the programmes and ideals of the different times and countries which have found symbolical expression in theories, and still more in pseudo-theories. This latter history is not distinguishable from the political or ethico-political history, as it is called, from the history of actions and events, with which it forms one; because theories, when they are tendencies cloaked as theories or armed with theories as weapons, form one with the will-in-action. A keen eye is undoubtedly needed to obtain from literary documents only what has a theoretical value in the philosophy of politics, and to extract from this only

E

the core and to follow its history. But those who do not tolerate a hotch-potch of theories do not wish to tolerate a hotch-potch of histories either.

Thus, to limit ourselves only to the examples already given, Hegel, in so far as he was the champion of Germanism and of conservatism, belongs to European history of the nineteenth century; but, for his new and historical concept of reality, he belongs to the history of political philosophy. Certain distinctions of his, if they do not have philosophical value, have value as empirical schemes and are pertinent to the history of political science. Similarly, Marx is an integral part of political history in so far as he expressed the sentiments, the hopes and the desires of the workers' movement; but he is to be placed in the history of political philosophy for his attempt to find a solution for ethics and any other spiritual form in economics; and in the history of political science for the emphasis he gave to the struggle of classes, to their ideologies and to the relationship between economics and politics. This does not rule out the fact, however, that for a full understanding one must never lose sight of the different facets of a person, both as writer and man.

Chapter III

ECONOMICO-POLITICAL HISTORY AND ETHICO-POLITICAL HISTORY

THE concept of moral history, which is, after all, precisely what is wanted and sought in the name of history, is a concept to be reinstated on the one hand and to be defined better on the other.

Actually, this term is not usually taken to mean the history of thought or of philosophy, nor the history of poetry or of art, nor agricultural, commercial or economic history, but precisely the history of the moral or civil life, whichever it may be called, of a people or of mankind in general. And this alone seems to be History, history *par excellence*. There are good reasons for this seeming to be so, although, strictly speaking, it is incorrect, since no form of history can be conceived which is sovereign over the others.

It will readily be conceded that that concept needs to be reinstated when one remembers the predominance of deterministic naturalism and of ethical utilitarianism in the general trend of thought in the second half of the last century and therefore in its historical writings, which had become almost completely oblivious of the moral spirit that inspires mankind (oblivious, one might say, of mankind). A type of dialectical view did follow that naturalism, but it happened to be in the form of historical materialism, which regarded economic life as the substantial reality and moral life an appearance, an illusion or a " superstructure," as it was called. The lowering of the moral conscience in historians continued even when historical materialism was modified and in part abandoned.

To confine ourselves to Italy, it is known that the young
school of historians of the beginning of the twentieth century
took delight in defining itself as an " economico-juridical
school," in this way excluding, or at least overlooking in this
definition, what should have been the principal aim of its
activity, namely, the representation and understanding of
moral life. Even to-day, the historian who places the account
of moral efforts and struggles above information about
economic matters and above descriptions of economic
struggles between social classes, is immediately classed as a
" literary man " or " philosopher," and not a learned and
expert historian. Just as I was among the first to recommend
the study of the concepts of historical materialism, which
seemed to me quite effective for awakening the lazy philo-
logical historical work of the scholars of that time and for
bringing it from words to facts, so I wish also to be among
the first to recommend that we rid ourselves of its residual
prejudices. This comes all the more naturally to me because
for thirty years I warned people against the metaphysical and
naturalistic presuppositions of that doctrine, and always
advised that its dictates be treated as simple empirical rules
of research.

In justifying this reinstatement almost as a *quaestio facti,*
one takes for granted its theoretical justification, that is, one
considers as solved the *quaestio juris* concerning the truth and
autonomy of moral activity against every utilitarian or other
kind of negation of it. Hence the logical necessity of a
history which will find its source and its subject in moral life.
Nevertheless, without in any way repeating the demonstration
of this essential point, known in philosophy as the basis of
morality, it will be permissible to say that a fresh proof of the
inadequacy which results from the exclusion, the neglect or
the insufficient emphasis given to the moral life, lies in the

dissatisfaction which accompanies the reading of histories that are purely or predominantly economic in character and are set up as integral histories. This is due to the feeling that there is something else, not told in those histories, something more important and higher, more intimate and essential.

But, undoubtedly, once the right and the necessity of moral history have been reaffirmed, it is equally urgent to determine exactly its content and, above all, to distinguish it from one of its false forms which has both masked and discredited it. I speak of what, to be correct, should be called not moral history, but moralistic history, because it exchanges and confuses the attitude of the moralist with that of the historian, which is totally different. The moralist, actually, is a practical corrector or censor who aims at maintaining a strong and inflexible moral ideal, and judges human matters from the exclusive point of view of *perfectio*, examining the correctness of single actions and the greater or lesser goodness of individuals. The historian, on the other hand, investigates the past in all its relations, in its logic and in its necessity; and, just as his sphere of interests is wider than that of the student of histories, so are his vision and his judgment; and also the scale of values which he follows, different. For this reason, he pays less attention to *perfectio*—to actions in all their innumerable details, to a series of beautiful actions, morally inspired and performed, or to praise of the goodness of the individual—than he does to the quality of the actions performed and to the meaning which they acquire in historical development. The best comparison to make clear this difference is that between the grammarian, or teacher of language and style, and the critic of poetry. The former—the usefulness and respectability of his task should be recognized and it is to be hoped that it will always be discharged diligently—scrutinizes exactingly the propriety and perfection of expres-

sions, praises the perfect ones and condemns the imperfect
ones; whereas the critic of poetry tolerates and even accepts
imperfections, provided he has before him a truly great
poetical work. The grammarians and teachers of literature
are inclined to approve modest and light writings in which
they find propriety and purity, but they also find fault with
and cast aside great works that are rich in virtues and not
lacking in defects, whence their well-known aversion to
Homer, Dante and Shakespeare. Similarly, the moralistic
historians, reducing everything to an equality by their criterion
of the moral *perfectio,* praise the mediocre but honest and
frown upon the great and guilty, the Alexanders, the Cæsars
and the Napoleons; or, searching intently for perfection and
rarely or never finding it in this poor world, which is always
in pain and always found wanting, they become tiresome and
irate, or gloomy and pessimistic narrators of the wickedness
and baseness of mankind. In confirmation of the double
characteristic here indicated, it is to be noted that moralistic
history increases and becomes predominant always in times of
discomfort and disaffection with human activities, civil and
worldly, and in the minds of those who are thus afflicted.
For this reason it had famous representatives, just as did
stoicism and other such ascetic philosophies, in the late
Græco-Roman era and above all in the times of Christian
transcendancy. In like manner the exclusive and tyrranical
domination of grammatical criticism and of the teachers of
literature belongs to the periods of little philosophical and
historical power and of little creative productiveness. Certainly we do not intend, as we have said, to minimize the
effectiveness of grammatical and moralistic criticism and of its
beneficent pedantry, nor to preach or promote a kind of
unbridled æsthetic and ethical romanticism. On the contrary, we intend, with the concepts explained above, to

recognize the element of reason which is in both types of romanticism, inasmuch as through its influence our attention is shifted from the small to the great and preference is given not to the small and perfect, but to the great even though imperfect. The graceful and polished literary composition and the elegant trifle are valuable things; but there are so many of them in this world, while there are so few *Divine Comedies, King Lears* and Medici Chapels. The humble and virtuous peasant girl may have as much moral value or even a greater moral value than the most powerful hero in history and she will go to Paradise, while the hero will go to Purgatory, if he does not go directly to Hell. But in the histories that are studied, narrated and meditated upon, that sinner will appear and be admired, whereas nothing will be said of the peasant girl.

Because moral history might easily be confused with moralistic history I have, on other occasions, designated moral history by a synonym, namely, ethico-political history, a term which has a greater chance of becoming accepted and less danger of being misinterpreted. This gives me the opportunity to explain, also, two important scientific forms in which this history has been presented in these last centuries, neither of which, in my opinion, is free from limitations and ambiguities, since each bears the imprint of the circumstances of the time and place in which it arose. It is known where, when and how the first of these forms, moral history conceived as history of civilization, arose: in the century of the enlightenment, in the Age of Reason, that is, of intellectual and abstract reason, and in France in particular. When one observes the kind of history against which it rebelled, there is no doubt that in its first impulse it intended to be a moral history, in the lofty meaning given to the word in this discussion, because it opposed history which was merely military and diplomatic, full of accounts of wars and negotiations, and emphasized the need for a more profound history, for a civil history of peoples. But the concept of civilization was quite vague and fluid and, instead of deepening the ethico-political content which it carried, it bowed to the needs of the times; and the resulting history took on the form of a history of the "diffusion of light" or of the "spirit of rationalism," as it was also termed. Whatever the other errors of that history might be, so far as concerns the part with which we are dealing, it is evident that it was limited fundamentally to a history of intellectualism, of positive science and of the successive decline of religious or mythological beliefs and of their superstitions. In short, it became, on the one hand, a mere history of thought, a theoretical history; on the other hand, a history of the spread and application of truths, that is, a cultural and practical history, to be sure, but not a truly ethico-political history; or, if it was such, it was a one-sided one.

In opposition to this conception of moral history as the history of civilization, which might be called a French one, arose the other conception which might be called German, of history as peculiarly political history, the history of the State, as the true, concrete and only ethical reality. This German conception had the merit of reasserting against the histories of the various economic activities, the history of the ethical activity which dominates and surpasses them all; and, also, of reasserting integral history against one-sided histories. It had the merit, too, of substituting for civilization the more profound and severe concept of struggle and activity in the State and for the State. But its fault lay in understanding ethics as the State in too narrow a manner, and in separating the State from the varied and complex life, both moral and political, which comprises both what is juridically termed the

" State," and what is termed the " Church," what is considered the State and what is considered society, what is
approved as the State and what is fought against as antistate;
in short, the positive element and the negative element, the
latter being in its own way positive also, *de facto,* if not yet
de jure. To this fault another is to be added, springing from
the country and the time in which that conception arose and
developed : the tendency to glorify as an ideal not only the
State of political men and jurists, but specifically the authoritarian and conservative State, which had guided the fortunes
of the German people.

Moral or ethico-political history must free itself from these
faulty theories and from these limitations of circumstance by
correcting itself and by conceiving as its object not only the
State, the government of the State and the expansion of the
State, but also that which is outside of the State, whether it
co-operates with it or tries to modify it, overthrow it and
replace it : namely, the formation of moral institutions, in the
broadest sense of the word, including religious institutions and
revolutionary sects, sentiments, customs, fancies, and myths
that are practical in tendency and content. If, however, one
wishes to consider the complex of all these movements as the
very life of the State, in its highest sense, we shall not object
to the word, so long as it is interpreted thus. In order to
assure this wider and more precise meaning, we prefer the
term " ethico-political " to the vaguer term " moral." The
creators of these institutions are the political geniuses and the
aristocrats or political classes which give them life and in turn
are created and supported by them.

In the sphere of moral or ethico-political history the other
histories pertaining to practical activity, the history of agriculture, of technical invention, of industry, of commerce, of
culture, etc., lose their autonomy and become part of moral

history; because the activities described by them are the
presuppositions of ethico-political history, instruments which
it uses for its own purposes, subject matter which it forms
and reforms. Such is also the history of wars, which in
ethico-political history no longer retains its own character as
history of military art, but is bound to moral life, inasmuch
as the character and the ethical virtue of peoples appear also
in war and in the preparation and pursuit of war. The same
is true with politics, understood in the narrow sense of the
word as the art of government and diplomacy.

But if it is claimed that those other histories find their place
in ethico-political history, this implies, at the same time, that,
taken by themselves outside that sphere, they follow their own
laws and should be treated differently, not only with a different breadth and particularization, but also with a different
approach. From the vague consciousness of the special
character of these histories and of their relative autonomy,
there developed the custom of adding, in history books, to the
principal subject matter, treated in such a way as more or
less to satisfy the needs of ethico-political history, a series of
chapters or additional readings on agriculture, commerce,
industry, military art, festivals and games, customs, literature,
the arts, science, philosophy. This type of historical exposition has been greatly criticized and satirized as history divided
into compartments or pigeon-holes; in spite of which it has
not been discarded, and in vain it has been and is asked to
give up its place to a unified history of all those matters. In
such a case the unification is actually impossible, because
those matters either become a part of moral history and are
moral history, as stated before, or they are treated and judged
according to their own criteria; they are then other histories
which may follow or precede that moral history, be bound
with it in the same volume, but can never become one with it.

Usually they are compilations of incompetent persons: chapters of literary and artistic history written without feeling for or comprehension of art, chapters of commercial or monetary history with which economists are dissatisfied and say, with reason, that " historians " (that is, " those historians ") know nothing about it and would do well to observe the motto, *tractent fabrilia fabri*.

If the chapters concerning the history of philosophy and of poetry and art, which belong to very definite histories of a theoretical order, are separated from these chapters, the remaining histories all become, even in their individual variation, a history of economic activity. In its strict and theoretical meaning, this history comprises the art of exchange and the art of political negotiations, the production of goods and of all other utilities, commercial competition and armed competition, which is called war. Differences remain between these various histories, and also in the varied preparation, experience and attitude required of those who write them, but they are merely differences of material, no greater than, nor different from, those which are found among the histories of poetry, painting, music, architecture, etc., all of them æsthetic history. The autonomy of economic history, in this comprehensive sense, is therefore to be restored in its relation to moral or ethico-political history; just as the autonomy of the history of art was restored in its relation to the history of thought and of philosophy.

It is, of course, a wholly dialectical autonomy, because the various autonomous histories are involved in one another; and distinguishing them does not mean division and separation, for this would make them all not only unintelligible but also impossible to produce, and would nullify them. But the importance of the re-established autonomy lies in making clear the impossibility of unifying them in another type of history, in which they would not be unified, but neutralized, and by which they would be nullified no less than by dividing and separating them. This autonomy would also show the impossibility of reducing any one of these histories to the one which follows or precedes it dialectically, and, in the present case, of reducing moral history to economic history or economic history to moral history.

This "moral" or "ethico-political history" (if I may be permitted this additional reflection) is, after all, what lies at the bottom of that frequently expressed assertion or postulate: that religious history is the true history of mankind. In this connection the following words of Goethe are usually quoted: "The real, unique and profoundest theme of the history of the world and man, the theme to which all others are subordinated, lies in the conflict between faith and disbelief. All the epochs in which faith dominates under any form whatever are splendid, encouraging and fruitful for contemporaries and for prosperity; and, on the contrary, all the epochs in which disbelief in any form whatever wins a poor victory, even though they may for a moment strut about in apparent splendour, disappear from the memory of posterity, because no one torments himself willingly to become acquainted with what is sterile." [1] Is not this faith, this impetus, this enthusiasm which distinguishes great historical epochs and peoples, merely faith in ethical universality? Is it not activity in the ideal and for the ideal, in whatever manner it may be conceived and theorized about, although always in some way speculated upon? Does it not have a metaphysical background in the invisible, that is, in the world of thought? In this connection, I remember that in the final years of the last century, when historical materialism was in full sway, a book which no one seeks or reads any more now, Kidd's *Social*

_____
[1] Goethe, notes to *West-östlicher Diwan*. Cf. *Israel in der Wüste*.

Evolution, caused a great uproar. In this book the author, a sociologist, a socialist, a Darwinian, or, rather a Weissmannian, even through this naturalistic and materialistic culture and preparation of his, came to the conclusion that social development and progress are in no way explained by the force of " reason," but only by the force of " religion." By a closer observation, it was easy to see that Kidd, following a certain English philosophical tradition, meant by " reason " the utilitarian calculus, and by " religion " the antiutilitarian (and therefore for him the irrational) acceptance of rules which are contrary to the interest of the individual as such, but foster the interest of mankind. This is equivalent to saying that the strength of social history lies in moral activity. We have already warned against confusing ethico-political or state life, which is the subject matter of history, with the State as it is conceived by purely political men for political or juridical purposes. Similarly, we advise against taking " religion " in the concrete meaning of the followers of the various religions or in the limited meaning of the philosophical adversaries of religions. Like Goethe, we should understand it in the sense of every spiritual system, of every concept of reality, which, transformed into faith, has become the basis for action and also the light of moral life. This last point is of some importance. Whenever religious thought or, better, thought in general, is considered not under this aspect of conviction and faith, and therefore not in its relationship to practice and transformed into practice, but as process, research, controversy and theology, religious history or the history of religion cannot be identified with ethico-political history, because obviously it belongs to the history of forms of thought and of the development of thought, that is, to the history of philosophy.

Chapter IV

LIBERALISM AS A CONCEPT OF LIFE

THE reader has probably been bewildered, or at least surprised, in following my discussion of the Philosophy of politics to find no examination of, or even reference to, so conspicuous a doctrine as liberalism, which has had, in the last two centuries, and still has so much importance in European history. In the preceding chapters the aspect of liberty has been defined as necessary in every form of life and as inseparable from the aspect of authority, which would not exist without it, because authority is to be found only with respect to what is alive, and only what is free is alive. Reference has been made to the liberal party, but simply as a party among parties, without any prerogative over others in the intricacies of political struggle, and subject to the same laws as all the others. The search for " the best state " has been discussed together with the other abstractions of natural law and so also has the definition of the liberal state as the best state; because every particular and historical form of state deserves to be born and to die, comes into being through opposition and struggle, and yields to new forms of government, which in turn involve fresh opposition and struggle. But the liberal doctrine, strictly speaking, has been left out of the picture that we have sketched. Why?

Because, actually, this doctrine goes beyond the formal theory of politics and, in a certain sense, even beyond the formal theory of ethics; it coincides with a complete idea of the world and of reality. Therefore, the failure to mention it before is not a denial of its importance but, on the contrary, an implicit way of admitting that it belongs to a different and higher sphere.

In reality, in it is reflected all the philosophy and religion of modern times, centred in the idea of dialectics, that is, of development which, by means of the variety and conflict of the spiritual forces, continuously enriches and ennobles life and imprints upon it its unique and complete meaning. This is the theoretical basis for the attitude of trust and favour which the liberal doctrine shows in practice toward all manner of tendencies. Rather than set limits and checks on these tendencies and rather than subject them to restrictions and repression, the liberal doctrine offers an open field so that they may compete among themselves and co-operate in harmonious discord. This idea of development from within, of immanence, springs from the criticism of the opposite doctrine, which, by separating God from the world, heaven from earth, spirit from matter, and ideas from facts, comes to the conclusion that human life must be moulded and controlled by a wisdom which transcends it and for purposes which transcend it. Above all, human life must be moulded and controlled by divine wisdom and by its interpreters and ministers, for purposes beyond this world. It follows that this attitude in practice, which is called authoritarian and distrusts spontaneous forces in conflict among themselves, tries to prevent or cut short the conflicts, prescribes the course to be followed and the methods to be used, and establishes the regulations to be obeyed. The authoritarian theory is by no means an immoral theory, *sic et simpliciter,* but a theory of another and lower morality, arising from other and inferior theoretical presuppositions. As such, it sees the liberal theory as its direct enemy. Against this enemy it is in a constant state of hatred and fear (to say nothing of its specific and solemn proclamations of war, or " syllabuses "); upon this enemy it always tries to inflict all possible harm, by incessantly hurling poisoned arrows and by incessantly summoning against it malcontents of the most varied types, taking advantage of every difficulty in which it is involved. This is as it should be; because the conflict between the two is without solution, inasmuch as it does not hinge upon particular matters, which admit of practical compromises, but on final matters, which do not admit of compromises. It amounts to a conflict between religions, in which the liberal doctrine of immanence proclaims itself to the authoritarian and transcendental doctrine as one who passes sentences and buries the dead, performing this task mercifully, and ready to accord all the honours due to the venerable being that is dead or near death; but in spite of this or, rather, because of this, it cannot expect to be received by the authoritarian doctrine with joy or resignation.

True, there are, or have been liberal-Catholics. We are not speaking of those who, prompted by the thought of over-powering liberty with liberty and of re-establishing the authority of the Church, tried in France and elsewhere to set up a party of this kind; rather, we are speaking of those others, men of good faith and high ideals, who figured so prominently in Italian history of the last century. These, however, never had the approval of the orthodox, nor did they escape contradictions within themselves. An example of such men is Manzoni, with his loyal and constant adherence to the ideal and to the realization of the independence and unity of Italy, and with a conception of history which is throughout moralist and pacifist, and fundamentally un-worldly. However, it is not our intention here to go into the complications of the individual conscience, but merely to point out the origin and the relation of pure ideas.

If the transcendental and authoritarian doctrine finds its

clear and logical formula in religious transcendence, it has also full right to lay claim to all authoritarian theories of political and moral life, and to the tendencies that go with them, theories which at first sight appear free of any reference to the world beyond and even deny and ridicule it. Such are especially the various " socialist " theories (without speaking of " the atheistic Catholicism " of the nationalists and the authoritarians of France and of other countries, and of similar preposterous or cynical manifestations). They establish as their ideal a paradise on earth, a paradise that is lost and to be regained (" return to primitive communism ") or a paradise to be conquered (" abolition of class struggles " and " passage from the realm of Necessity to the realm of Liberty," according to the Marxian interpretation of Paradise), a paradise described as an arrangement of reason or justice. This ideal cannot be translated into actuality except in so far as one wishes to impose it ready-made. It has as its basis the idea of " equality," understood not as the consciousness of common humanity, which lies at the bottom of liberalism itself and of all true ethics, but as quality conceived in a mathematical and mechanical way. Nevertheless, under these crude and materialistic forms, this ideal hides the enduring appeal of the idea of a realm of perfection without diversities, made up of beings who are all equal before God; indeed, if this implied and unconscious reference were removed, the ideal would soon appear empty and meaningless. Again, socialism provokes the hostility of the liberal doctrine precisely because of this substantial negation of struggle and of history, because of the authoritarianism to which it is forced to cling and which it sometimes calls " dictatorship " (wishing to make every one hope it is temporary), and because of its inevitable inclination to stifle the diversity of impulses, spontaneous developments and the formation of individuality. Thus a

F

further conflict, one which takes on the religious character already mentioned, arises between socialism and the liberal doctrine. From other particular postulates of socialism there does not arise a conflict of principles, because liberalism neither has any reason to oppose the ever greater humanization and the increasing dignity of the working classes and of the workers of the soil (in fact, in its own way it aims at this goal); nor does it have a bond of complete solidarity with capitalism and with the system of free enterprise. Liberalism can certainly admit varied systems of arrangement of property and production of riches, with the sole limitation, on the sole condition, with a view to ensuring the unceasing progress of the human spirit, that none of the means chosen will prevent the criticism of what exists, the search for and the discovery of improvements, the putting into effect of these improvements; that in no one of them should we try to create the perfect man or the perfect automaton, and that in no one of them should we take from man his human faculty of erring and of sinning, without which not even good can be done—good as each one feels it and knows he can do it. In these respects liberalism seems at times to become one with democracy and at times to be divergent from it and in conflict with it; liberalism is in contrast to democracy, in so far as democracy, by idolizing equality conceived in an extrinsic and mechanical way, tends, whether it wishes to or not, towards authoritarianism, towards a static State and towards transcendence, that is, in so far as it is or contains socialism. But liberalism seems to become one with democracy in so far as the latter opposes other forms of authority and in so doing is liberal and can lend a helping hand as an ally. For this reason the wavering position for which liberalism is rebuked in its relationship with democracy is seen to be nothing more than the wavering nature of the latter, which is liberal toward certain old or new authoritarian regimes, but no longer liberal or not liberal enough toward certain others. For example, it is liberal toward theocracies and absolute monarchies, but it is not liberal in its liking for the social republics (which are no less theocratic, even if they are materialistic); and it is severe toward rulers and the ruling classes, but weak, as it were, toward the man in the street. From the point of view of liberalism, which has always been against the theory of equality, liberty, according to one of Gladstone's sayings, is the means of creating and promoting aristocracy, not democracy. Aristocracy is truly vigorous and serious when it is not a closed but an open aristocracy, firm in rejecting the crowd, but always ready to welcome those who have raised themselves to its level.

Liberal thought and the liberal spirit, by means of the associations and unions which circumstances require, create for themselves corresponding institutions in the form of liberal practices or of the liberal state, as well as of the party or parties so called, which confront and combat the parties seeking to overthrow them : the reactionaries and the revolutionaries, the retrogrades and the ultraprogressives. Nevertheless, although these parties are usually separated into these two classes they are all, in so far as they are antiliberal, fundamentally retrogressive and antirevolutionary. When they get the upper hand, they bring about reactions, not revolutions, as in the " Brumaire 18ths " and in the " December 2nds," which no historian considers revolutions. Only liberal uprisings bring about real revolutions. Whereas an authoritarian regime, once it is overthrown can never more be resurrected as it was before, because of the indelible changes that have come over persons and interests, the liberal state alone seems to rise again time after time, always with the vigour of youth. It seems so, but in reality it does not rise time after time; rather, it never dies. It is the only type of state capable of " restorations." Its recurrent death is apparent only. In that apparent defeat and submission, we have in reality the defeat of a form of reaction (the so-called " license," that is not liberty, but tyranny of the few or of many) by another form of reaction, " just as a nail is driven out of a board by another nail " : a reaction which the liberal method, in certain historical circumstances, had not been able to control and direct. But the victorious reaction has but one guarantee for consolidating its victory : to negate itself, and to return to the liberal method. In other words, its victory is assured by giving of its own strength to the liberal method, which needed new strength, by giving it support and then withdrawing or, more often, by urging it on with stings and blows, and by inducing it to produce something new, as the plough does the earth. Reactions are always crises and illnesses, and the liberal regime stands for health and vigour. For this reason mankind in its heart never has any love for times of reaction and for the leaders of reactions, however great they may have been. When confronted by Metternichs or even by Napoleons, men are puzzled and ask : " Was his true glory? "; but their hearts are filled with admiration and love for the times of liberty and for those who established or restored liberty. But the liberal mind, the liberal concept, does what the heart of humanity cannot do : in the role of historical judgment (and no longer as the foundation of the actual conflicts of life), it finds a logical explanation for reactions and their leaders. In this sense the liberal mind regards the withdrawing of liberty and the times of reaction as illnesses and critical stages of growth, as incidents and steps in the eternal life of liberty; and therefore it understands the purpose that such times have fulfilled and the useful task they have accomplished. Here we have clear proof that the liberal concept is superior by far to the authoritarian; the latter is not able to justify theoretically and historically the former which, on the other hand, justifies the opposite doctrine, and makes it a part of itself by transcending it. Histories written by reactionaries of all kinds, whether clerical, feudal, Jacobin, socialist or nationalist, are always extremely passionate and biased, bitter and pessimistic; they are always presented in the form of conflicts between God and the devil, between reason and irrationality. On the other hand, histories written by liberals, the offspring of the historical intuition of modern times, minds which have been moulded and trained for history, remain impartial and attain serenity of judgment; because in the most varied, conflicting and violent pages of history, they see only men, men in their various tendencies, and with their various vocations and missions; and they see only reasons against reasons, and if they see the devil, they see him only as Fontenelle suggested, namely, as " *l'homme d'affaires du bon Dieu.*"

It has frequently been observed by many that the idea of liberty which I have sketched above, that is, the liberal concept, is an entirely modern one, foreign to the ancient and medieval world, which knew liberty only as the right of the citizen or as the privilege of this or that class; that is, to be more precise, as liberty related to laws and guaranteed by laws and contracts. This observation is not only true, but to us who have recalled the philosophical presupposition of modern liberty, it must indeed seem obvious, because it narrows down to the general statement that modern philosophy is not ancient or medieval philosophy; that the historical concept, which is now innate in moderns, is not the naturalistic or theological concept of antiquity or of the Middle Ages. It might be shown in this instance, as has been shown for philosophy in general, that there do not exist any clear demarcations between antiquity, the Middle Ages and the modern era; and that both modern philosophy and the liberal concept are foreshadowed and prefigured in earlier times. By way of illustration it is enough to recall, with regard to the liberal concept, the sublime longing of the ancient heroes for liberty, and to recall Christianity with its new concept of humanity and of the history of humanity, and chivalry with the sentiments of mutual respect it fostered among warriors of different faiths. But, on the other hand, all this would confirm their modernness, in the sense of their flourishing and expansion in the modern era, after the Renaissance and the Reformation. The research that has been made recently into the genesis of the liberal concept in Calvinism is of considerable value. It is useful in clarifying the moral-religious character of that concept and in distinguishing between Calvinistic liberty, founded on the idea of inequality and of the special vocation of each individual, and the doctrines of natural law. The mechanical equality of the latter represents, rather, the origin of the democratico-socialistic concepts, contradictory and inherently liable to change to authoritarianism, as in Hobbes' natural law. But one must not, by exaggerating the results of such research, forget that all of modern philosophy, with its historical attitude and with its dialectics, no less than with the ethico-theological speculations of Calvinism, had a part in the formation of the liberal viewpoint and tendency, whose tie with modern philosophy has already been pointed out; and it still has a part in it to-day, with its later developments and resolutions. When, at the beginning of the eighteenth century, Shaftesbury said, with patriotic delight, that his England had then attained " good taste in government," he certainly was not restating the *de optimo statu* problem, but was giving proof of the ideal of the new times, which had there raised on high its flaming torch.

Therefore, whenever we hear (and we heard it frequently) the liberal point of view labelled as " formalistic," " empty," " sceptical " and " antagonistic," we should turn this accusation against modern philosophy, which is more directly affected and which answers it with all its power. For modern philosophy has given up the claim of ever being " definitive " and has therefore given up all dogmatism, being satisfied, on the other hand, with remaining perpetually alive and able to state and solve all the problems that arise *ad infinitum* in life, and able to develop dogmas perpetually, without ever nullifying them, but making them always deeper and larger. The liberal conception, as an historical conception of life, is " formalistic," " empty," " sceptical " and " agnostic," like modern ethics, which refuses first place to laws, casuistry and charts of duties and virtues, and places the moral conscience at its centre; like modern æsthetics, which refuses models, categories and rules, and places at its centre the genius that is good taste, both sensitive and very strict. Just as this æsthetics does not wish to be subservient to schools, large or small, but to interpret the aspirations and works of original and creative spirits, so the liberal conception is not meant for the timid, the indolent and the pacifist, but wishes to interpret the aspirations and the works of courageous and patient, of belligerent and generous spirits, anxious for the advancement of mankind and aware of its toils and of its history.

Chapter V

CONTRASTING POLITICAL IDEALS
AFTER 1870

WHEN in the romantic and realistic era the idea was formulated that the history of humanity is nothing but the story of liberty, there was thus established both a criterion for interpreting the history of humanity and the ideal or religion immanent in it.

Is it possible to substitute a different concept for the concept of liberty, or at least to complete it and go beyond it to a loftier concept? At first sight, it would seem so, in virtue of a logical doctrine which was in vogue at that time, namely, that each successive philosophy uses as a phase of its own the constructive principle of the preceding one. And it would also seem so on the basis of fact, because, especially from 1870 on, scepticism and open rebellion broke out against the ideal of liberty when other different or opposite ideals were exalted and preached; and apparently all the most recent history has followed or set out on other roads.

Let us examine first the logical justification. We must recognize that the doctrine to which we have referred was later cleansed of whatever remained in it that was *a priori* or intellectualistic. Criticism was directed against the conception of the history of thought as a sequence of closed systems, each with a principle superior to that of the preceding one; and the conception was modified so as to regard history as a perpetual germination of new problems, which are born of its own movement and of the movement of life as a whole. That is to say, a truth, provided it is a truth, can never be supplanted, but is, rather, enriched by new truths and set in new relations. The truth of Plato or of Aristotle, of Christianity, of Vico or of Kant has not been refuted or put on a lower plane, but it lives perpetually in us, breathing more freely in a wider world.

Let us examine the actual facts.

It is commonly admitted that events which took place in 1870 and after shook the faith in liberty, considered as a means of checking, satisfying and harmonizing new needs, and of gradually solving the difficulties inherent in preserving the social order and promoting progress. The unification of Germany had just been accomplished, not through liberty, as was hoped in '48, but through the efforts of a military state and of a minister who scoffed at liberalism and had given the German people a constitutional, but not a liberal government; that people, nevertheless, showed self-confidence and distinction in all fields. Other states, like Austria and Russia, which stood self-condemned in the light of liberty, proved to have strength and vitality, and were sought after and courted as allies by liberal nations; others, like Turkey, were tolerated or even flattered. The people's indignation against the Bulgarian and Armenian massacres was dulled by the hard and unyielding hearts of statesmen whose names were Bismarck and Disraeli. Having cast aside the utopias of " Young Europe," of the " United States of Europe " and of the " Holy Alliance," the nations had armed to the teeth against each other; they struggled to secure markets; and they all gained or sought territorial acquisitions outside Europe, in Africa, in Asia, in Australia. Political parties were formed and reshaped, less according to idealistic principles than according to certain economic tendencies, and all appeared directed largely by economic matters. Economics itself no longer trusted in free enterprise, but obtained protective provisions, and provided its own protection by forming leagues of industrialists in order to maintain profits at a certain level. The State took on an ever increasing number of tasks, in contradiction to the theories of liberalism. As a counterpart, rather than as an opponent, of political Bismarckism and of industrial plutocracy, the workers' movement was growing, under the name of socialism, akin to the other movement in emotions and ideas, with the exception that the one derided liberty as " a thing for idealists " or for " ideologists " and the other as " a bourgeois lie," and both idolized the force of the fist. The Catholic Church, which the Illuminists and the rationalists had believed near death and which the religious souls had futilely thought of saving by means of an evangelical revival, was gaining political strength, especially among the rural classes; and governments counted on her, for she had on more than one occasion helped them ward off the danger of upheaval. Culture became dyed with materialism or positivism, placing natural science and mathematics at its head in place of philosophy, which had reigned there in the past. This very trend left the way open for a revival of mysticism, for reaffirmations of the transcendent, and even for the restoration of Thomism and of scholasticism, irreconcilable with modern philosophy, but not with the positive sciences. Social power passed from men of ideas and ideals to those economically important, whether they were plutocrats or proletarians, and to their mouthpieces. Historical materialism, substituted for the religious history of mankind, was the theoretical projection of this attitude of the spirit. While awaiting the dreaded or hoped for social revolution or its prologue, historical materialism was apparently fulfilled in World War I, a war that was wanted by no one, yet was prepared and fanned by all, and soon proved to be so thoroughly devoid of idealistic motivation that it was popularly called a European " conflagration " and not a war. The literature of the periods preceding and following the war, a sensual, pessimistic literature which praised violence or was fascinated by it, reflects the change which had occurred and forms a contrast to the literature of the preceding era.

This, in brief, is the picture of the new era as described in the English, German, French, Russian and other histories and which is becoming the accepted account, emphasized and repeated by all. We do not intend to deny its external, partial or one-sided truth, and certainly we do not deny that after 1870 faith in liberty was sharply assailed and shaken. However, whether a faith is contested and shaken or not is not the essential point which determines its validity. Indeed, by its very nature truth must accept and defy doubts and attacks. It never dies as a result of these; when it does die, it dies only of itself, when it is revealed to itself as contradictory and not true. Both the means and the seal of this dissolution lie in the fact that the fallacious truth is replaced by another truth, which is not fallacious or is less fallacious. Therefore, the essential point is not to be found in the perplexities, luke-warmness, disbeliefs, negations and obloquy, which are the lot of almost all truths, but in the validity or falsity of the idea that has taken its place.

From this point of view, let us examine the ideals or counter-ideals opposed to that of liberty in the development of recent history. Though they are hailed as being invested with all the qualities which the theory of liberty seems to lack —seriousness, reliability, reality, universality, and saving efficacy—we fail to discover any that will really withstand criticism and we are almost bewildered by so much ado about nothing, by so large a mountain giving birth to such wretched intellectual abortions. Foremost is the doctrine of the struggle for existence and of the survival of the fittest, which inspires the political ideology of both communism (with its class struggle and dictatorship of the class powerful in number and expert in the material production of the means of subsistence) and imperialism or nationalism, which transfers the same struggle from social classes to peoples and states. This doctrine is found in a heroic and aristocratic form in that kind of troubled religion named after Nietzsche, a poet with an anguished heart. Its weakness is revealed in its bitter clash with the moral conscience, to which it is utterly abhorrent; the moral conscience feels that sad, indeed, is the image of human life which is postulated by it and which it overshadows; and vile, indeed, that man who is condemned to make slaves and become a slave, to die and to spread death fruitlessly, with no promise of happiness other than that of the horrid sneer which gladdens the temporary oppressor of classes and peoples or, what is little different, the æsthetic excuses of a Nero. If, in order to defend this ideology, we temper and correct it, linking it to the moral conscience, as a struggle which is not closed in itself and sterile, but which has as its goal the ever greater moral advancement of man, with the hero acting as the creator of good; if, thereby, we somehow illuminate and clarify the process itself of the struggle, we are gradually brought back to the concept of the struggle for liberty, which implies contrasts and antitheses, does not object to rebellions and wars, when they are necessary, and does not shrink from suffering and from the blood that man has always shed in order to make the history of mankind bear fruit. The restoration of the bad copy to the condition of the good original is rather analogous to the return which criticism brought about of naturalistic evolutionism to the theory of dialectic development, of which it was a distortion or debased symbol.

Having considered this counterideal, which has fared better

than all the others in practical life and in literature, it is sufficient to deal briefly with that ideal which aims, for the sake of the salvation and peace of mankind, at the re-establishment of religious transcendence in the form of obedience to the Catholic Church, to her teachings and to her ethical and political dictates. In order to put into effect such a system it would be necessary to undo the entire history of civilization and even the history of Christianity and of the Church, which form an integral part of history. And it would be necessary to erase this history of many centuries, almost as though it were an incorrect sketch, and substitute for it a static doctrine, fallen from heaven by way of the mind of some priest or moral theologian. The desperate nature of such an undertaking is seen in the fact that the Catholic Church, still strong and anything but negligible as a political element, is completely unproductive in the field of thought and culture, though she partially succeeds in concealing her aridity in these fields by borrowing methods, ideas and results from lay thought.

Finally, it hardly seems necessary to do more than mention the æsthetic, the anarcho-nihilistic, the ascetic or Buddhistic counterideals. If in modern society the two ideals examined above have as their support, the one the intoxication of bloody excess and productive impetuosity, and the other, the pride of an ancient and still surviving Roman-medieval tradition, these other counterideals are mere fantasies of amateurs, individual caprices or freaks of childish spirits. Not even deserving of the name of counterideal is that other tendency, equally childish, which longs for the ineffable, always expects the *quid novi* and the wonderful, and despises the existing ways of feeling and thinking in comparison to some non-existent way, which it finds beautiful because it is non-existent.

If from this glance at counterideals we pass to a consideration of the innumerable doctrinal polemics directed against liberalism and democracy; and if we concentrate, as we should, on the fundamental meaning of the discussion and on its conclusion, and not on particular criticisms, which can be and often are justified, we always observe one of the two following cases: (1) that those polemics are not conclusive or constructive and are therefore insufficient in themselves and at best mere satirical outbursts of bad humour on the part of reformers who do not know which way to turn, or (2) that they conclude that it is convenient to correct and improve the present procedure by making the liberal order ever more effective and less fictitious and formalist. Thus the directive idea or principle, since it cannot be replaced by another, remains beyond controversy, and the question is transferred to the most suitable means of its attainment. Hence the proposals for checking the abuses of the majorities, the tyrannies of parties and the intrigues of politicians; for avoiding the deceptions that envelop the masses; °for stressing the title and the responsibility of the ruling minority or political class and of its leaders, as against the myth of the People; for adding checks to those which are already in existence or in place of those which do not serve the purpose; for removing certain pseudoliberal superstitions, which are no longer applicable to the new conditions and sometimes hide interests that are illegitimate or have become illegitimate, etc. All these proposals take for granted the moral conscience and the good will of men;- from which they proceed, as means and instruments, and by which they are created. If this presupposition did not have a solid foundation, if, as is commonly alleged, men were inherently stupid and mean, there would no longer be any need to think of an organization of liberty or of any other organization, and the only thing left would be to hope for a universal fire which would consume a world no longer worthy of life. But this is so much talk or jest. The fact remains that moral enthusiasm at times is kindled and at times damped, at times springs forth with energy and at times relaxes from habit, comfort and the policy of *laissez.faire*. It is therefore necessary, in lay society as well as in the Church, that from time to time apostles, martyrs and saints intervene; these certainly cannot be made artificially, but must be trusted to Providence, which will continue to send them on earth, as it has always done. For this reason, many think that the fundamental problem of our times is a religious one; I, too, am of this opinion, but with the added comment that the problem of all times is religious and that our problem is not a matter of inventing a new religion for our times, but of making ever stronger and more profound the existing religion, which once used to be called inborn or natural religion and now might be called historical religion.

The impossibility of erasing or replacing in the minds of men the concept of liberty as an ideal and as a directing principle is ironically confirmed by the fact that even Napoleon I said at Saint Helena that he intended, in the end, to give liberty to France and to all Europe; that Napoleon III conceived it as the crowning feature of the edifice that he was building; and that Bismarck, fallen from power, proclaimed, in a well-known speech to the students of Jena in 1892, his distrust in absolutism and recommended that the efficacy of public opinion and of the parliament be increased. Let us take a more recent example, from World War I: when it was desired to warm the hearts of the suffering peoples at war, the light made to shine before their eyes was the liberty and the alliance of peoples: that liberty which they would have awakened everywhere, even among their enemies reluctant to accept it, and that alliance of peoples, or league of nations, for the peaceful and free development of world civilization. If the tongues that preached these things were often false, nevertheless that ideal was the only one that could be defended, the only one that could be resorted to with certainty of good results.

We seem thus to have come to a strange example of divergence between theory and fact, between idea and reality, because those counterideals which do not hold good in theory and are found to be irrational are confirmed, and that ideal, which alone can be confirmed by reasoning, is denied by the history of the last sixty or seventy years. One might almost say that the history of philosophy and of political doctrines follows a road that is different from or opposed to that of civil and political history. But the apparent divergence can only make us doubt that this history has been well understood, a doubt that has already been implied, with the reservation that the usual historical picture resembles reality only apparently, extrinsically, or one-sidedly. Represented in this way, history has appeared at times as a decadence (how much talk and how much boasting of decadence there has been in our times!), at times as a negation of the history of preceding eras. On the contrary, it is neither the one nor the other, but simply a continuation and, if we wish, a laborious continuation. In other words, that period which has been described as one of departure from the liberal ideas can be understood only as the struggle of those ideas with the new events and the momentous developments which these ideas were called upon to dominate. Had the romantic, idealistic and liberal age, perhaps, given permanent order to society, or directed it to the royal road along which it would have proceeded thenceforth without obstacles and difficulties? The romantic age had, in fact, simply made more evident a great guiding principle, had made men more conscious of it and had used it more or less successfully to solve certain problems of its time. And as usually the case, the romantic period added hasty generalizations, slogans (" let the colonies perish rather than the principles!"), false hopes and that kind of mythology which so easily attaches itself to each new truth. It was not surprising, then, that the struggle should continue or become more bitter, that difficulties should arise that had not been experienced before or not to such an extent or degree, that illusions should be cleared away, generalizations revised and corrected, and mythology replaced by criticism. Thus in the field of economics free enterprise ended, after being over-simplified and becoming a sort of optimistic belief in a general cosmic harmony. In international relations the limitations of the movements toward national unity were perceived, and it became obvious that the equally romantic politics of the Restoration and of Mazzinianism had to settle its accounts with reality and learn something of the old politics, that had been rechristened *Realpolitik*. In the newly-formed states it was learned that national unity might be accomplished without achieving a liberal regime, and that the one might precede or follow the other. In internal politics it appeared that the parliamentary vicissitudes were not always sufficient to guarantee social harmony. In ecclesiastical politics it was felt that rationalism and anti-clericalism had not the strength to abolish and destroy the Catholic Church and, indeed, were introducing the danger of depriving society prematurely of one of its strong forms of organization and order; it was also felt that the lay religion, which had grown in the eighteenth and nineteenth centuries, was not yet mature enough to avoid inclining now toward materialism and now toward the old faith, to avoid pessimism or a feeling of solitude and of tediousness; it was apparent that humanitarian proceedings could not be applied to uncivilized or partly civilized peoples, for whom the old right of conquest and of subjugation was in force. Finally,

G

to mention, as we have done before, the realm of culture, it was seen that the attractive idealistic philosophy, with its *a priori* constructions of logic, of the world of nature and of the world of history, had also been in some parts oversimplified, and the necessity was recognized of reinstating with honour and relative autonomy the positivist sciences and philology. It is not surprising that, in making these corrections and admissions, theorists should go too far, carried away by the argument that free enterprise should be denied in theory, and that with it the nationalistic movement, parliaments, freedom of thought, humanitarian feeling, the effectiveness of morality, and idealism as such, should be denied. All these negations were made easy by the fact that the things which were denied were enjoyed, were useful and made life and action possible for those who denied them. On the other hand, economic forces were very powerful and the contrasts between capitalists and proletarians, between employers and workers were thereby sharpened. These forces are by nature economic and not ethical, and they know nothing of the government of society, of the actual course of history or, in short, of the needs of the human soul. It was quite natural that the merely economic theorists should turn their desires either to rebuilding society completely, from its very foundation, against its own nature, or to re-establishing authoritarian regimes in spite of history; it was quite natural that they should find men of letters and thinkers ready to echo their desires and to set up communistic or absolutistic ideals, dressing the latter with the rags of old history, as though with magnificent garments and glorious banners.

However, throughout these contrasts, these difficulties, these exaggerations and these vociferations, the principle governing the history of the age we are treating is always the liberal principle, because no other has arisen or shown constructive strength.   Even in the prostration produced by World War I, the greatest and most destructive ever seen up to that time, communism or pseudo-communism was put to the test only in a country that had remained outside the liberal world; and perhaps it will there finally open the way to that life of freedom that the preceding autocracy had not been able to produce.

Let us resume our retouching of the historical picture of the period following 1870.   We must realize that the theory of free enterprise has not been refuted but made more profound, more vital in the spirit though not in the letter, and that in spite of its errors; though it has had to withdraw in certain directions, in which it was encroaching unduly for the sake of material gain at the expense of national, state and moral values; though it has not prevented the intervention of the State or of municipal administration in economic affairs, nor forestalled the great body of social legislation.   Even when free enterprise has lost ground in international commerce because of the prevailing interests of certain States' and of certain classes, it has found compensation in the greater area of new States and empires, and it still remains the star from which we are compelled to take guidance and direction.   The long struggle in France for the establishment of the liberal republic first against legitimists, Orleanists and clericals, and later against the dictatorial and reactionary attempts of Boulanger and of the Dreyfus affair, developed victoriously in the decades after 1870.   As in the case of France, which had suffered the lesson of the Second Empire, the liberal regime has likewise remained unshakable in the countries where its tradition was older and where (as Hegel would say) it had transformed itself into a *Vorurtheil* or common conviction and had become life and blood.   It should also be observed that the highly praised unification of a great people through military power and through exalting the *raison d'etat*, independently of liberal forces and liberal education, has proved to be quite lacking in stability, according to the opinion of the keenest intellects of that same people. The latter, after a painful experience, has shaken off princes and princelings, the founders of that unity, and has formed itself anew with a liberal organization. It should also be observed that the only one of the large European state formations which restrained national individualities has crumbled. The socialist movement, which seemed so threatening at the close of the last century, at that very time and in that very country which had formed its theory and philosophy, came suddenly to a famous " crisis " and, being opposed to internationalism, later led to the most definite nationalism. Elsewhere socialism was gradually becoming a parliamentary struggle, into which it was introducing new men, new forces and new concepts. Colonial imperialism has already extended the liberal organization to other parts of the world; and, with the modern civilization which it introduces everywhere, it promises to continue to extend them, to a greater or lesser degree, in the more or less distant future. The idea of the " Holy Alliance " and of the " Young Europe " reappeared and tried to create a medium suitable for itself in the League of Nations.

Finally, to return once more to the cultural field, philosophical idealism, which is one with the liberal concept of life, seemed crushed under the heavy obstacle of naturalism, positivism and scientific principles, all associated with the authoritarian concepts or leading to them. On the contrary, shaking off the stones and the fragments, it has risen again, in recent decades, stronger than before because it has become more expert and wiser. And everywhere it is regaining domination in the world of thought.

The process is still going on, with greater difficulty than

before, because World War I, the first world " conflagration," solved far fewer problems than was hoped.   In fact, it seems to have aggravated them all, if this aggravation itself is not the sign of an approaching solution, that is, of the entrance upon a period of relative settlement and respite, not of a peace that is undisturbed and without conflicts, which cannot be a reality or even an ideal for man.   It is not for history to make forecasts, though fools ridicule it and call it useless for its failure to do so.   Its function is quite different : to show what has really happened, to show what the present really is, an epilogue of the past, containing in itself the life of the past, in order to establish through clear understanding of the past, the foundations on which our proposed structure must be built.   The nature of the moral duties which the history of our time prepares for us is easy to perceive from this inter-pretation.   Moreover, at the conclusion of this interpretation, there is implied the historian's patient willingness to wait.   If the historian's interpretation of the function of history is incorrect, let it be revised, corrected, and reversed by research and reason—in short, by the historian's own methods.

Chapter VI

FREE ENTERPRISE AND LIBERALISM

THE economic formula of free enterprise [1] has the same character and origin as the political formula of liberalism and, like it, results from the immanent and historical concept of life already explained. An economic parallel to the authoritarian claim to determine beforehand how men should think and act politically would be the claim to determine similarly the " just " price of anything. Both claims are medieval, even though they may be made again in each new era, even in our times (after all that has happened in the interim, our times should be considered somewhat distant from the Middle Ages). Both are opposed by liberalism and free enterprise which are paralleled, in the field of science, by the formula of free research and free discussion, that is, by the idea that truth is not something ready-made, but a perpetual becoming ; not a thing, but a thought, in fact, thought itself. Historians show how all these and other analogous and related liberties have become conscious of themselves and how they have been forming and asserting themselves in juridical institutions throughout the modern era.

There is, then, no difficulty so long as we limit ourselves to recognizing the working of one principle in the different spheres of life. But the difficulty appears as soon as we give to the system of free enterprise the value of a norm or of a supreme law of social life ; because in that case it is placed next to ethical and political liberalism, which is also declared

[1] Croce intentionally uses two terms having the same root, *liberismo* (free enterprise) and *liberalismo*, to show that free enterprise and liberalism are related, yet different. (Translator's note.)

the norm and supreme law of social life. Of necessity, a conflict arises. Obviously, two laws on the same level to cover the same matter are too many: there is one too many. Unless both prove faulty, one of the two must supersede the other or, better, merge the other with itself. If this merging is carried out by the law which is entitled to supremacy or exclusiveness, all is well; if by the inferior law we have an attempted usurpation.

This is exactly what happened when the status of a social law was assigned to the system of free enterprise, which was thus changed from a legitimate economic principle to an illegitimate ethical theory, to a hedonistic and utilitarian morality. This morality erects as the criterion of good the greatest satisfaction of desires as such; that is, of course, in spite of the apparent plural, the satisfaction of the pleasure of the individual or of society, taken as an aggregate and average of individuals. This tying of free enterprise to ethical utilitarianism is well known, just as it is known that utilitarianism, in one of its forms as made popular by Bastiat, tried to idealize itself as a general cosmic harmony, as a law of Nature or of Divine Providence.

Let us put aside Bastiat's philosophy, which, though its logical basis has never been properly criticized, is now certainly not only abandoned but forgotten (though it should not be forgotten because it is a typical form of a mistake apt to reappear). In the uncalled for elevation of the principle of free enterprise to the rank of a social law lies the reason for the apparent need to reject the principle itself. In fact, to those of mere utilitarian satisfaction the demands of morality are regarded as superior needs; to the averages of utilitarian satisfaction, to the more or less extended and general quantity there is opposed quality, that is, the qualitatively moral. Nor can the difficulty be overcome by determining the spheres of what is to be allowed and what is not to be allowed, because even this statement of the problem is faulty in the light of ethics, which ignores or refutes the concept of what is " allowed," of what is permissible or legitimate. When we try to test the demarcation of the two spheres in practice they overlap, and it becomes evident that either everything or nothing is permissible.

The difficulty disappears when we recognize that the supremacy belongs to ethical liberalism and not to free enterprise, and when we treat the economic problems of society in relation to ethical liberalism. The latter shrinks from the authoritarian regulation of economic activity in so far as it considers this regulation a suppression of the inventive faculties of man and, therefore, an obstacle to the increase of prize possessions or of riches. In this respect it moves, as is natural in view of their common theoretical root, along the same lines as free enterprise. But it cannot accept as prized possessions only those which satisfy the pleasure of the individual and as riches only the accumulation of the means for such an end; and, more precisely, it cannot, from this point of view, accept without question that these should be prized possessions and riches if they do not all serve as a means to the advancement of mankind. The " liberty " of which liberalism means to speak is intended to promote spiritual life in its entirety and, consequently, only in so far as it is moral life.

Once this is established, the problem for liberalism consists in determining, according to time, place and a given situation, not whether a certain provision is " merely or abstractly economic," but whether it is " liberal "; not whether it is qualitatively productive, but whether it is qualitatively worth while; not whether its quality is pleasing to one or many, but whether it is beneficial to one person, to many or to all, to man in his strength and dignity as man.

It may be—in fact, it is true—that in this examination liberalism approves many or the majority of the demands and measures of free enterprise, to which modern civilization owes so many benefits; but liberalism approves them not for economic reasons, but for ethical reasons, with which it sanctions them. For the same reasons, it rejects or restricts, in other cases, certain other demands which, under the name or appearance of liberty, are obstacles to liberty or, to use quantitative metaphors, are obstacles to a larger liberty in favour of a smaller liberty. This is not a negation but a confirmation of free enterprise, and at most it is the negation of utilitarian morality, by which free enterprise allowed itself in the past, and still allows itself at times, to be contaminated. Moreover, what we are trying to present in clear critical terms may be said to be recognized by the economists themselves, even if in a form which is too little critical and exact. These economists (with the exception of a few fanatics, chatterboxes and popular propagandists who deal in simple ideas and superficial statements) have always admitted that the principle of *laissez faire et laissez passer* is an empirical maxim, which cannot be taken in an absolute manner and must be limited. However, the limit is here understood as something placed *ab extra* and, as such, is a contradiction of the concept which we thus intend to limit; hence, either the concept itself is destroyed or the limit is rejected. The true limit is the inner one, which is no longer the limit of the concept, but the concept itself made more profound and, as we said, confirmed.

If the economic measures and regulations which liberalism disapproves of and fights against are only those that oppose moral development and progress (and they can be so judged only when they take on a concrete form), it follows that all the theoretical discussions about this matter are abstract and lack solidity. Only practical discussions are of value, such as are developed and decided in the actual fullness of life. The theoretical discussions, for example, will revolve about what field should be left to the activity of the individual and what field should be left to the action of the State. But, economically, what is the State if not the individuals themselves in certain forms of association, and how can their respective spheres be determined? On the other hand, the practical discussion will deal with the nature of a given provision, as to whether it is liberal or not, morally good or bad. Let us take another example: there will be theoretical discussions on the two different and opposite economic systems, the system of free enterprise and socialist system, and on the preference to be given to the one or the other. But in what respect are these two economic systems different and opposed in reality? What economic provision in the system of free enterprise is there that could not be called socialist in part, and vice versa? Here again, on coming to the core of the matter the discussion centres about good and bad, about better, not so good and worse, from the civil and moral point of view. It will be quite possible, with the most sincere and keen liberal conscience, to support measures and regulations which the theorists of abstract economy classify as socialist; it will even be possible, using a paradoxical expression, to speak of a "liberal socialism," as I remember is done in a beautiful English eulogy and apology for liberalism by Hobhouse. Serious opposition in principle to socialism only arises when it is a question of upholding liberal ethics and politics against the authoritarian ethics and politics which lurk at the basis of socialism.

Chapter VII

THE BOURGEOISIE: AN ILL-DEFINED HISTORICAL CONCEPT

HAVING experienced in my reading of the works of modern historians a feeling of dissatisfaction and frustration aroused by their use and abuse of the term "bourgeoisie," I have finally decided to give expression to my growing conviction that we must get rid of that particular use of the term.

I am speaking of a use in its specific context and not in other contexts, not, that is, of other legitimate meanings that may be expressed by the same word.

Thus the juridical use of "bourgeois" is perfectly legitimate as we find it in medieval history and even in some centuries and in some countries of modern history as long as it refers to the citizen of the town and of the non-feudal city, or the component member of one of the "states" of the ancient political order. In like manner the economist's use of "bourgeois" can be legitimate when it refers to the owner of the tools of production, that is, of capital, as opposed to the proletarian or wage earner. It is true that in this second instance it would be better to substitute the more correct term "capitalist" and not let the matter be obscured by confusion over secondary characteristics, leading to the customary inclusion among the bourgeois and exclusion from the class of proletarians and salaried men, of professional men, scientists and men of letters, because of their ways of life and the nature of their work. Economically, the difference between them and the so-called workers is non-existent or indefinite. Finally, it will be well to grant that in a social

sense the name " bourgeois " can be given to the man who is
neither too high nor too low, to the man who is " mediocre "
in feeling, habits and thought.

The historical use of " bourgeois " and " bourgeoisie " which
I am criticizing and denying is, on the contrary, the one in
which by " bourgeois " and " bourgeoisie " is meant a complete
spiritual personality or, correlatively, an historical epoch in
which such a spiritual formation is dominant or predominant.
Here it is no longer a question either of a juridical or economic
matter, or of an empirical social distinction, but of a moral
matter.   Inasmuch as each morality has at its foundation a
theory of life, it is also a question of a type of religion or of
philosophy, of a number of convictions and ideas which, even
though they may not be static but in movement and therefore
changing and developing, follow a general direction and obey
one principle or a set of principles of their own.   In modern
historical writings the term " bourgeois " is widely used with
this meaning, and it is made the subject of research in special
monographs, such as that by Sombart in 1913 [1] and that by
Groethuisen in 1927. [2]

In the meaning defined above it may be said that the idea
was misbegotten, that is, born not of a purely historical consideration, but of a practical polemic: of an economic,
political and moral controversy carried on by two opposing
parties against the society and the new ruling class which
emerged from the French Revolution.   On the one hand, the
new social form was looked upon with scorn and sarcasm by
the aristocrats and the supporters of the old regime, who hated

---

[1] Sombart, Werner, *Der Bourgeois, Zur Geistesgeschichte des modernen
Wirtschaftsmerchen* (München ed., Leipzig, Duncker and Humblot,
1920).
    [2] Groethuisen, Bernhard, *Die Entstehung der bürgherlichen Welt und
Lebensanschauung: I: Das Bürgertun und die katholische Weltanschauung* (Halle, Niemeyer, 1927). French edition: *Origines de l'esprit
bourgeois en France. I: L'Église et la Bourgeoisie* (Paris, Gallimard, 1927).

it both from prejudice and motives of self-interest. On the other hand, it was looked upon with envy by proletarians and workers. The mouthpieces of the latter or, rather, those who insisted on becoming their interpreters and representatives—that is, the socialists who appeared at that time—on comparing this social form with their ideal of a communistic society, condemned it in the name of the more or less immediate future, just as the former (the aristocrats and the supporters of the old regime) condemned it in the name of a more or less remote past. And both helped to form the conception of " bourgeois " and of a " bourgeois epoch of civilization," colouring it with shades to match their feelings of aversion and the purposes of their polemics. The formation of this pseudo-historical and intrinsically polemical conception took place in France in the first half of the nineteenth century and bears the French imprint in the word itself, which, in its corresponding forms in the other languages, took the French meaning in addition to the old meanings. In German, since *Bürger,* the word which corresponds linguistically, does not lend itself to the new meaning of the word and is therefore considered somewhat inappropriate, there is sometimes an outright substitution of the French form *der Bourgeois,* in which form it appears in the title of Sombart's book. Perhaps the man who contributed most to that pseudo-historical conception and to the new use of the word was Saint-Simon, who seems to have summed up within himself the two opposite aversions of the old aristocrat and of the new apostle of socialism. Thus there crept into modern historical works the idea of " bourgeois " and of a " bourgeois epoch," ranking at first on a level with conceptions such as the " Roman era," the " Classical era," " Christianity," " Catholicism," " Protestantism " and the like, and then gradually invested other superior qualities, as though it were the hidden motive

of the spiritual forms of the modern era. The analogous
motives of ancient economy and of ancient civilization in
which slavery existed, and of medieval and feudal economy
and civilization, in which serfdom and closed corporations
existed, were correlated with the motive of the spiritual forms
of the modern era : a final elaboration that was the outcome
of the increasing socialist polemics and, of the still more
energetic pseudo-scientific and pseudo-historical form which
then took in Marxism or historical materialism. Moreover,
even to-day, in all Europe one observes in the use of that term
the double trend which created the conception, that is, along-
side the socialist, communist and even anarchist trend, the
aristocratic and reactionary trend, which finds expression in
the various nationalisms, accompanied by dreams of absolutism, and of nobility to be reinstated, and of Catholic
discipline to be re-established.

It is to be noted that while in the sphere of social and
political controversies and in the country in which they were
most lively and outspoken there arose the conception of the
bourgeoisie as a spiritual figure and as an historical epoch, the
highest form of modern history which was derived from the
idealistic philosophy, especially in Germany, completely
ignored that conception and felt no need of referring to it.
On the contrary, it conceived of history as the history of
thought or of religion or of the development of consciousness,
and the like, and divided it into eras which mark the various
stages of this development, such as Theocracy, Classicism,
Christianity, Humanism, Reformation, Rationalism, Illumin-
ism, Romanticism, and so on ; and, when the pride of the
various peoples entered into it, the history was divided into
such eras as the Greek, the Roman, the Latin, the Celtic, the
Germanic, etc., with each of these " spirits of peoples "
(*Völkergeiste*) taken as the conveyor of spiritual values or of

systems of these values, which are more or less complete or are consecutively progressing toward completeness.

Because of the polemical and false origin of the conception of which we are speaking the method usually used in its analysis by modern historians is to be judged as ill-founded and not very intelligent. This method consists in trying to find what exactly are the characteristics of the *bourgeois* and of the age in which he predominates, and how the age began and what is its course, thus presupposing the reality of that figure and that age. Rather, it would be well in each case to re-examine the presupposition itself, and at least to cleanse it of its polemical refuse and correct it in a critical way, not even excluding the possibility that criticism will lead directly to its dissolution, which indeed is my thesis.

On the one hand, the aristocratic and reactionary polemic seemed to identify the bourgeois with the capitalist, with the speculator, with the enriched shopkeeper, and then also with the politician, with the demagogue and with other types which became well-known figures in novels and comedies. On the other hand, this polemic, when examined in its innermost content and taken in its relations and in its entirety, reveals itself as the negation of the whole civilization that has been maturing in the modern era. It was opposed not only to the exaggerations, deficiences and crudities which are found in every man and in every society of men, which vary in quality according to the different societies, and which it is necessary to fight against and hold in check, it was also opposed to modern philosophy, which had defeated and taken the place of theology. It was opposed to criticism, which had destroyed and was continuously destroying dogmas; to liberal governments, which asserted themselves against authoritarian governments, to parliaments which had succeeded courts and state councils; to free enterprise which had forged its way against mercantile and protective systems; to the transference of wealth from one person to another, as against the keeping of wealth in the same family through inheritance, *fidei commissa* and other ties; to the new methods which were upsetting old habits; to the needs for new comforts, which were tearing down old castles and other buildings and were reconstructing and enlarging old cities; to the democratic way of life, which measured man by the single standard of pure humanity, that is by the standard of the power of the intellect and of the will; and so forth. And quite often, this polemic spoke clearly: beyond the " bourgeois " or in the " bourgeois " taken as a symbol it singled out, as the chief enemy, modern rationalism, incredulity or disbelief, and individualism, and blamed the great men, Luther and Descartes, Calvin and Bacon, Voltaire and Rousseau, and also Kant and Hegel, and all the rest. Therefore, to accept the conception of " bourgeois " and of " bourgeois era " meant getting caught in the snare set up by this pseudo-history. Such a pitfall could have been avoided and still could be avoided if the cards were all put on the table: and under the bourgeois type, drawn more or less satirically and made disagreeable or comical, the serious character of the whole modern era was made clear. Against the modern era as thus presented, trivial attempts to discredit it are of little or no value. And the fact that the modern era was hated and ridiculed by the reactionary polemic and simply denied by its historians, proved the weakness of this history, that is, its pseudo-historical quality, because true history does not deny but justifies, does not reject but explains, does not know any bastard and degenerate children, but only legitimate children. These legitimate children, whether they are liked or not, will in turn have their own offspring—offspring that may even please those who criticized their parents and who, in so doing, helped to form the character of the offspring, and became spiritually another set of parents.

Socialist criticism and history had no part in the mistake of rejecting and denying the so-called bourgeois era and civilization as being the embodiment of extreme degeneration, because it wanted to express the thought of a revolutionary age, not of a reactionary one, and therefore it did not want to go back but beyond the present and the past. Hence, in opposition to the fantasies about the natural state of mankind, of the golden ages and connected utopias, socialist criticism and history took on the form of anti-utopian or critical or scientific socialism, and of economic determinism, or historical materialism, different names being used at different times. Its different attitude is proved by the sketch of the bourgeois era contained in the *Communist Manifesto* and by the almost lyrical or epical eulogy with which this concluded. However, if on the one hand, socialism avoided the anti-historical attitude of the reactionaries, on the other hand it fell itself into an error of historical judgment. In socialism, too, the bourgeois was presented as a decidedly economic reality; but, although he was satirized in his exaggerations and deficiences, in his vulgar and coarse aspects, in his crudity and hypocrisy as profiteer, like the bourgeois described by Fourier and like the character whom Marx called "the knight of the sad face," he could not be restricted to that narrow role. In socialism, too, the conception of the bourgeois era was expanding and was becoming the conception of the whole modern era, of geographical discoveries, of industry, of machines, of protestantism, of rationalism, of the encyclopædists' and of the Kantian philosophy. Socialism meant to go beyond the modern era not only with a different system of economic production, with the abolition of private capital, but also with a complete transformation of thought and of customs, with a

H

new philosophy, a new morality and a new art. It does not matter that socialism should, with an arbitrary and fantastic assertion, make all these things depend on the economic order and vary as functions of it; because what matters is that these other things, too, should be included by socialism in its vision and in its predicted and desired revolution. Historical materialism wanted in fact to be a new philosophy and not a mere economy (the book *Capital* is but a part of the vast work conceived by Marx), a doctrinal motive that should find its place in a new vision of reality and of life. Engels tried to develop historical materialism along these lines, especially in his *Antidühring*—the same Engels who proclaimed the proletariat to be the direct " heir of the classical German philosophy " (i.e. conserving, negating and superseding it), and who came close to postulating a proletarian ethics, and even a proletarian logic, dialectics, theory of knowledge and, I was about to say, mathematics! In Italy, Antonio Labriola worked along these lines for many years; while Sorel dreamed of a new morality and new customs, the seeds of which, according to him, would have been sown and cultivated by the workers' sydicates, similar in this respect to the primitive Christian *ecclesia*. Not every one has forgotten the illusions, kindled everywhere, even in Italy, some fifty years ago, of a socialist science and a socialist art, as opposed to bourgeois science and art, already scorned in the name of a present looking to the future. If any one has forgotten them, what the Bolsheviks attempted ingenuously in Russia, with their educational institutions and with their " schools of poetry," would help to reawaken the memory.

But the fact remains that this new proletarian philosophy, religion, morality, customs, science and art were empty desires and not reality, words and not concepts; and they could not defeat the corresponding bourgeois systems, as one can perhaps admit, at least in idea, occurred in their economic system of production, because those bourgeois systems are not merely bourgeois or economic, but human in various ways, and therefore speculative, æsthetic and moral, and they can be superseded only in their own sphere and for inherent causes. In their own sphere they are continually being super-seded and transformed, becoming richer and more detailed, without ever an indication of abandoning their governing principle, which has been taking on a more definite form during the entire course of history. During the Middle Ages and immediately after, and especially later, between the eighteenth and nineteenth centuries, the governing principle of these systems seemed to be an outright reversal of the old principle, whereas it was actually a process of strengthening it and developing it dialectically. In the light of this increased strength it was possible to speak with some reason of a " new " or " modern " era, and the aristocratic or Catholic reaction-aries were able to point out its chief characteristics and to detest it. But the socialists, who carry on and want to give added impetus to the modern era, cannot lower it to the level of a spiritual era already passed; they cannot have recourse to anything that may be analogous to the real Catholic-feudal-authoritarian-theocratic past, of which the reactionaries availed themselves as an ideal and as a criterion of judgment for the creation of their pseudo-history. The modern era recognizes its socialist elements and features, just as the Jew of Bernstein's drama recognizes in the champion of anti-semitism the child of his blood, endowed with the same passion and with the same psychology.

After these remarks it does not seem necessary to add other arguments to show the inadequacy, indeed the emptiness of the conception of " bourgeoisie " as a substitute for that of " modern era." Nor does it seem necessary to point out how

timely it would be to advise the historians to avoid the use
of the term bourgeoisie with the meaning of modern era, as a
frequent source of distortions, misrepresentations and biases
in their descriptions and in the processes that they explain and
illustrate. I would almost say that they must drop that word,
leaving it to the polemics of reactionaries and socialists, or use
it as little as possible, that is, only for certain aspects of past
and present life to which it belongs, or only as a metaphor,
accompanied by the consciousness of its merely metaphorical,
image-producing and expressive function. And even the
liberal men of politics should guard against that word, realiz-
ing that to accept the polemic conception of " bourgeois " as
scientific truth is like unconsciously accepting the anti-liberal
ideology, whether reactionary or socialist, with which, when
used in this way, it is deeply imbued (hence the saying that
" liberty " is a " bourgeois ideology," that is, an ideology of
economic defence, and that " idealism " is a " bourgeois
philosophy," etc.). But, although our demonstration is now
complete, it will be useful, as an added proof, to consider
briefly the books we mentioned on the history of the
" bourgeois " and of the " bourgeois era."

For example, what did Sombart wish to do? The sub-title
of his book reads: " a contribution to the spiritual history
of modern economic man " (*Wirtschaftsmensch*). However,
the *homo œconomicus* cannot have a spiritual history, but
only an economic one; and therefore that spiritual history is
of the " modern man," but not of the " modern economic
man," who, as such, cannot under any condition be " the
representative bearer (*der repräsentative Träger*) of our time,"
as he is said to be in the preface of the book. With this confused and contradictory initial concept, it is not surprising that
the history written by Sombart is an accumulation of many
facts and of many explanations of certain groups of facts;

but it leaves a " disquieting impression," [3] as the author himself admits, because it lacks a clear development. After having made this admission, Sombart tries to justify it in the light of the "infinitely complex" nature of his problem; of the critical caution which makes him flee from the general " easy formulas " (*bequeme Formeln*) of explanation; of the "multiplicity of causes," which he was obliged to pass in review; and of his refusal to resort to a *causa causarum* in the manner practised by historical materialism.[4] At most, he says, one can postulate a general order for principal and subordinate causes, with a sort of hierarchy of causes, such as would be, after the fall of the Roman Empire, the two powerful impulses of the search for gold and of the spirit of enterprise, from which resulted modern institutions and even the modern State, and with it the great stimulus to the capitalistic spirit. This stimulus is represented as the heresy which presupposes the religious need at the bottom of the European soul. All this led peoples away from their own countries and to the founding of colonies. Taking on forms ever more free from violence and becoming ever more commercial, the spirit of enterprise gradually spread from the barons and warriors, who were first to be filled with it, to large groups of peoples, especially to the Etruscans or Tuscans, to the Frisians or Flemings and to the Jews. Professional militias, the authority of moral forces and especially of religion, the mixture of races increased it; until capitalism, which, until the end of the eighteenth century was still bound by moral ties and by ties of tradition and religious creeds, freed itself of all bonds. The science of the Romano-Germanic peoples contributed to this unlimited development, as did the capital created by the Jews, the influence exercised by the latter on European economic

---

[3] Sombart, *op. cit.*, p. 457.
[4] *Op. cit.*, p. 459.

life, the weakening of religious sentiments and the breaking down of all obstacles in foreign relations, an act which facilitated the emergence of economic forces.[5] But what Sombart calls, in this history of his, the lack of a single line or of an " easy formula " is a lack of the logical sense, that is, insufficient mastery of the matter on the part of the thought; in truth, a complete mastery was impossible since the point of departure lay in a confused conception. If he had cleared up that initial conception he would have been confronted with the history of the modern spirit, more or less the same as that treated by Dilthey in his well-known book [6]; and he would have been able to enrich it and to define it better in its details, and, above all, to expand it from the history of ideas and theories to the history of common feeling, of customs and practices and of industry. And he would have made a real contribution to the spiritual history of modern man, including the industrial phase in so far as it ties up with this history. The centre was always to be sought in the intellectual-moral movement.

Sombart himself, when speaking of the precapitalistic economic life, puts the matter very well : " All its single traits, like those of cultural life in general, find their intimate unity in the fundamental idea of a life that is based on the perseverance and the working of men side by side in space. The highest ideal of that time, as is very apparent from the wonderful system of St. Thomas Aquinas, is the single soul which is closed in itself and rises to perfection from its very core. All the exigencies and ways of life are adapted to this ideal. To this corresponds the strict classification of men in professions and states, which are all considered of equal worth in their common relations with the whole and which offer to the

---

[5] *Op. cit.*, pp. 459–62.
[6] Dilthey, Wilhelm, *Weltanschauung und Analyse des Menschen seit Renaissance und Reformation* (Leipzig, 1921).

individual well-defined forms, within which he can develop his individual being toward perfection. There also correspond to it the directive ideas to which economic life is subordinated, the principle of working to do what is required of necessity and the principle of traditionalism, both of which are principles of perseverance."[7] One does not understand why, having connected medieval economics with medieval philosophy and ethics, he did not proceed in the same manner in the study of the modern era, and why, in his new navigation, he threw away that good compass. It would have even freed him from the alternation of fear and bewilderment by which he is assailed when he glances at the future of the bourgeois and capitalistic spirit : fear and bewilderment arising from the fact that he separates that spirit from the spiritual whole to which it belongs and in which it finds both its stimulus and its check and from the fact that he conceives it as a sort of violent force of nature, a " giant," as he calls it, which is now in the flower of its strength. As long as this strength lasts, what else can be done, he says, but make provisions for protecting the worker's body and life? But will it last? It is to be presumed that it will not. Signs of fatigue are already visible in certain tendencies toward the comfortable and the luxurious, and in the increasing bureaucratic centre of enterprises; and other signs will probably appear, such as the decrease in the birth rate. But what will happen at the weakening of the capitalistic vigour? " Perhaps the giant, having become blind, will be put to pulling the cart of democratic civilization; perhaps, too, we shall have the twilight of the Gods. The gold will then be put back into the depths of the Rhine. Who knows?"[8] These are neither historical nor ethical questions. The man who, with the historical and

---

[7] Sombart, *op. cit.*, p. 23.
[8] *Op. cit.*, pp. 413–14.

ethical sense, is in the struggle of life does not ask himself these questions. He is concerned with promoting the eternal elements of health and vigour which are in the only civilization that is called, as has been pointed out, " modern " merely because of an empirical distinction from the ancient and medieval civilization. After the first of these civilizations it seemed that civilization was declining when actually it was becoming deeper and wider; and after the second, there seemed a complete inversion of the preceding civilization and it was instead a more intense continuation; indeed we still feel that we are heirs not only of the Greek and Roman spirit, but also of the Christian.

Groethuisen's book does not enter into the thorny problem of the universal historical construction, in which Sombart is caught, because he studies only the rise of the bourgeois spirit in France. In his first volume he studies only the relation between this spirit and that of the Church in the seventeenth and eighteenth centuries. It is a very interesting work because of the subject treated, which comprises things to which the lay world rarely turns its attention, that is, sermons, religious instructions, books of religious morality and of criticism and discussion of the customs of the time, and the like; and it is very interesting also for the very clear manner in which it is written. But not even Groethuisen, when he describes to us this bourgeois spirit, succeeds in showing that his historical picture is the picture of a " class." This spirit begins to form its own idea of things as opposed to the ideas of the Church. It behaves in a lukewarm, indifferent and unbelieving manner with regard to the dogmas. It turns away from the other world and looks only at this world. It is no longer clouded and darkened by the idea of death and of the world beyond. It is no longer troubled with the sense of sin. It no longer considers work as a suffering and a punishment, but as a duty,

a source of joy and pride.   It cultivates a " positivism of life "
(*ein Lebenspositivismus*) and has, in short, a new ethics of its
own, different from the Christian and ascetic ethics.   And
so Groethuisen. goes on in all the details which he cleverly
brings to light. He himself repeatedly considers the bourgeois
" our manner of being, thinking and acting," the " dominating type of the modern era," and whenever he makes some
weak attempt to stamp this type as a class type he does not
succeed in his effort.   Thus he will observe that the bourgeois,
in spite of his lack of faith and his mental independence,
mindful of keeping the people in check and therefore, having
become prudent, "intends to reserve his morality for himself
and, as for the others, they can remain believers until further
notice."   And he will judge that " this is enough to show us
how closely the new morality, whatever the generous forms
with which it is adorned, is related to the spirit of a class." [9]
But prudence, it seems to me, belongs to all builders who do
not remove the scaffoldings and supports when the building
is not yet in a state to stand on its foundation (indeed
Groethuisen himself says " until further notice ").   Even
though prudence may sometimes become hypocritical and
degenerate into a class expedient, in itself it has nothing to
do with class spirit.   There would have been little doubt
about the matter if the bourgeoisie or the directing or liberal
class, of which it is here a synonym, had ever followed a
programme of keeping people in ignorance and in superstition, as was done by reactionary governments; whereas the
fact remains that it made a part of its programme, and
provided for, the education of the people precisely by means
of those lay principles which were its very own.   The idea of
the God-policeman, which belongs to the reactionaries and

[9] Groethuisen, *op. cit.*, French ed., p. 293.

to the old aristocrats, appears among the component elements
of the bourgeoisie in an entirely individual or episodical way,
and it is felt as a decline of the very vital principle of the
bourgeoisie, as a betrayal of its own ideal and as a break in
its own tradition.   Therefore, in spite of the fact that the
classification of " class " spirit appears here and there (but
very rarely) in Groethuisen's exposition, the image which he
paints is not that of the bourgeois, but that of modern man
in general.

Nor does Groethuisen succeed in the other attempt which
he makes of separating in some way the formation of the
bourgeois spirit from the spirit of modern philosophy.   In
this attempt he insists on pointing out that the way of being,
thinking and acting of the bourgeois, his *Weltanschauung* or
concept of the world, is a " fact " and not a " thought," such
as that which philosophies usually accomplish; and he gets
his material from the sources we have indicated, which are
books of churchmen, of preachers, of spiritual directors, not
of philosophers. If it is a *Weltanschauung,* for this very same
reason it is a philosophy; if it coincides, as it does, with the
modern philosophy of immanence, it is this philosophy; if
the books from which the proof is taken are not written by
philosophers, it means that philosophical matters are not
found solely in the books of those who are philosophers by
profession and are interested in establishing their system; and
if, finally, it is a problem not only of philosophy, but of a way
of life, it means that it is really a problem of philosophy, of
serious philosophy, which is at the same time a way of life,
and gives to life and takes from it in a circular process that is a
unity. At most, the profit that Groethuisen derives for philosophy from so-called non-philosophical books lends further
proof to a favourite thesis of mine, which is precisely to understand philosophy not in a bookish and scholastic way, but as

thought, wherever and however it is expressed.[10]   Did not Jesuitism with its education and its casuistry, and Jansenism with its concept of grace, have a part in the formation of the modern mind and spirit; or did they have a lesser part (what does " lesser " mean here?) than that of Rousseau with his social contract and than that of Kant with his assertion of duty?

In the historical studies and in the political science of to-day other serious traces might be indicated of the confusion introduced between the meaning of " class " given to the word " bourgeois " and its meaning of spiritual totality which goes beyond class distinctions.   We may mention, at least, Kay Wallace's theory [11] of the " twilight of politics " in our day and in the near future.   Politics would disappear because the powers of the world are now the industrialists and the workers, the plutocracy and the proletariat, whereas the "middle class " or bourgeoisie, which was the class that did the thinking and made politics, is increasingly crushed between the two enormous antagonistic forces, and the modern world no longer moves according to politics but according to economy.   Now how can any one think that a spiritual category, essential to humanity, will ever disappear?   How does one arrive at such a strange idea?   The cause of this error is precisely the identification of " politics " with the bourgeois class, with the " middle class."   But it can be said that in the words themselves is indicated the refutation of the error, because the *bürgerlich* is also the " civilian," and the " middle " class is also the " mediating " class; that is, it is not an economic class, but the representative of " mediation " in utilitarian and economic struggles.   This mediation has not been actualized, and is never actualized in any way other than by surpassing

[10] Cf. Croce, *Teoria e storia della storiografia* (Bari, Laterza, 1927), pp. 145-146.

[11] Wallace, William Kay, *The Trend of History* (New York, Macmillan, 1922): *The Passing of Politics* (London, Allen and Unwin, 1924).

and therefore refutating that struggle by means of ideas that are no longer economic, nor ideas of mere, crude politics, but ethico-political ideas, as they are usually called. Therefore, the "middle class," of which we are speaking here, is a "class not a class," similar to that "general class," to that *allgemeine Stand*, to which Hegel granted the "general interests," *die allgemeine Interessen* [12] as a sphere of activity belonging to it and as its own business. I say "similar" and not completely "identical" because Hegel, letting himself be influenced, as elsewhere, by the conditions of the Germany of his time, attributed economic stability to that class from the comforts granted to it by fortune or the stipends furnished to it by the State, and he assigned it solely to the "service of the government" (*dem Dienst der Regierung*). However, the bourgeois or middle class must be understood more widely and in its pure sense as comprising those who have an ardent desire for the public good, who cherish a passion for it and sharpen and define their ideas to this end, and act accordingly. They are rare at their best, but they are surrounded by many lesser figures, in whom the same passion and the same thought are found, and who help them. They are as rare as poets, great poets, but not, because of this, solitary and ineffective, because they diffuse poetry in the hearts of the people around them.

Thus by starting from the completely prosaic conception of the "bourgeoisie," we have come close to poetry. In this way we intend to have definitely separated the bourgeoisie in its spiritual meaning, the bourgeoisie that is so called through an ill-chosen metaphor—an interpretation of bourgeoisie which is often substituted for the other and which, what is worse, unfortunately contaminates the other, to the detriment not only of historical judgments, but also of sound moral and political judgment.

[12] Hegel, *Philosophie des Rechts*, pp. 205 and 305.

Chapter VIII

THE UNENDING STRUGGLE BETWEEN "STATE" AND "CHURCH"

LEOPOLD RANKE used to say that history is always the history of the relations and struggle between Church and State—a saying of profound truth, which it is worth while to clarify and make more specific.

Certainly we must not think here of Church and State in the sense of two historical institutions which, as such, have been and still are the object of special research on their relations, their conflicts and the different settlements of these conflicts, with now the one now the other institution prevailing. I confirm the observation, which I have made elsewhere, that such a history, after all, can be understood only as the history of two forms of State, one of which tends to subordinate the other or even to make it a part of itself. According to the times, the one or the other can be the champion of moral and civil progress. Therefore, the dualistic or eclectic criteria, which envisage the two institutions as in a state now of armed peace, now of good neighbourliness, now of separation, are inadequate for such a history. These criteria, rather than being the criteria for history, are its subject matter; that is, they refer to the vicissitudes and temporary settlements of those conflicts.[1]

If we wish to discover what is profound in Ranke's saying we should think, instead, of the Papal encyclical of December, 1926, which protests against the " concept which makes of

[1] Cf. Croce, *Storia della storiografia italiana nel secolo decimonono*, Bari, Laterza, 1927, II, 95–96.

the State the end and of the citizen, of man, the means, monopolizing and absorbing everything in the State," a concept which, according to the encyclical, "cannot be the Catholic concept." Whatever the application and the practical aims of the encyclical may have been, the Pope was right in the theoretical statement, which is irrefutable; because what was vindicated by him against the State, in the symbol of the Church, was nothing more or less than the moral conscience.

It was a merit of the Catholic Church that, to the best of its ability, it asserted this exigency against the crude and one-sided Machiavellianism, that is, against the theory that mere politics is a thing complete in itself, and that, by the unrelenting pressure of its opposition, it forced this theory to correct its exaggerations and distortions, to advance toward completeness and truth, always retaining that particular initial truth which was its own.[2]

But the conflict between State and Church, between conscience and political action on the one hand and conscience and moral action on the other, is expressed not only in that Catholic form, but also in a number of other different forms which it would be worth tracing and collecting: such as the Vichian conflict between "certain" (in a practical meaning, that is as an assertion of force) and "true" (in a moral meaning); and also, the conflict, typical of the eighteenth century, between *politics*, which deals with state and war, and *reason* or *civilization*; and finally, understanding *civilization* in a disparaging sense as a number of useful and practical conveniences, the conflict, in German thought, between *Civilization* and *Kultur*, and so on.

Many times (not only in the Middle Ages and not only by

[2] For the effectiveness of the anti-Machiavellianism of the Counter Reform in the development of the theory of State and politics, see Croce, *Storia dell'età barocca in Italia*, especially Part I, Ch. II.

the Church) there have been attempts to oust the State with the help of the Church by reducing everything to an abstract morality; and at other times the State has tried to oust the Church by reducing everything to a function of the State or force or economic interest. These attempts to exclude one of the two are reflected in historical writings.

But the attempt of the one to oust the other meets with no success. Each of the two opponents rises again after having been crushed in vain, and both appear anew as if bound together; with the Church perpetually correcting and subjugating the State, but taking it for granted and preserving it even while correcting and subjugating it.

If the State is imagined as the earthly and diabolic element and the Church as the heavenly and divine element, then it must be said that heaven cannot exist without the earth, nor God without the devil. But, actually, both are human forces which harmonize in their connection and in their dialectics the unique process of human volition and action: life which is elevated to morality and morality which is transformed into life.

There are times in which everything seems to be force and politics, utility and labour: times of poverty and hardships, or of frenzied mammonism, of tyranny and slavery; during such times the religious and moral spirit, as well as the poetic and speculative spirit, can hardly breathe. Yet, that spirit is never absent and inactive; even the empirical prevalence of the political element, or State over Church, is to be interpreted as the formation of something which the ever triumphant Church will dominate and bend to her own purpose. For this reason, as every one knows, the pessimistic historians are always wrong; in fact, they are not historians at all.

From the point of view of the historian it is absurd to suppose that the moral flame which burns in the heart of humanity has ever been or can ever be extinguished—the flame which gives the historian the very light by which to understand events. It is not absurd, however, to find such a belief in the moral conscience, which is what it is because it is always afraid of being overcome and lost, because, as the Gospel says, it is always "fearful." And the moral conscience not only fears, but laments, considering itself lost in the individual as well as in the world, and stays frightened and moans until religion or her sister philosophy intervenes to give it new solace; from the convulsions of this anguish, which reappears periodically, which cannot be suppressed and which it would be fatal to suppress, a great part of the sublimest poetry is born.

Hence we perceive the sophistry of those who, actuated by baseness and cowardice, change the theoretical and historical point of view into a practical and moral one, and conform and advise conformity to the facts, because facts, they say, are the only concrete morality, and everything else is imagination and empty pretexts. As if the problem were the historical one of understanding the facts and not, as is actually the case, the ethical problem of changing them, that is, of creating new facts. These persons indeed try to break one of the most delicate springs of morality: like someone who would cut away from the physiological organism something which he thinks superfluous, but which nature has created and placed there for the economy and the harmony of the whole. And whenever we hear someone refer to "historical necessity" rather than to his conscience to justify an impending decision about some line of action, we can be sure that we are faced with a case of lack of moral sensibility, or with an attempt to defraud the inescapable law of duty.

The perpetual struggle of "State" and "Church" which is waged in history, and the impossibility of suppressing one of the two opponents, is reflected in the distinctive vocations and attitudes revealed in all walks of life. Thus, in the field we are now considering, side by side with men of action, politicians, warriors, leaders of industry and commerce; side by side with the busy-bodies, the underhand and the unscrupulous; side by side, that is, with every kind of worldly person—from highest to lowest, from master to servant, from aristocracy to rabble—we find Churchmen who help the weak, rebuke, condemn and anathematize the oppressors, bring souls back to eternity and to God, mitigate the fierce contrasts and direct them to a good end, adore and pray, announce and prepare the ways of the Lord. The term Churchmen must be understood as is the term Church, in an ideal sense, as including those who, in modern and lay society, are represented by the worshippers of truth, by those who increase their own and others understanding, by the custodians of ideals, by all those who, like the ministers of religions, have the care of souls. It is to be observed that no objection is raised when individuals are occasionally seen departing from their particular occupation or changing it completely, so long as they are not wasting themselves in sterile caprices and so long as the change brings fruitful results. Moreover, when men whose behaviour has been merely utilitarian act thus, suddenly assuming a moral role, expressing ideas on words not expected of them and accomplishing generous actions, that particular change of occupation is greeted with profound satisfaction. On the contrary, we feel profound disgust when Churchmen, lovers of truth, teachers, custodians of ideals, play the parts of politicians, of violent men, or traffickers, of intriguers, of gendarmes and of executioners. In this case the change of role is considered a backward step; and inasmuch as no moral reason can justify such a step, it is clear that it has as its motive some kind of profit for the individual, and it

I

narrows down to an apostasy, a desertion, a betrayal, a failing in honour. Ordinarily, these deserters carry on even their new trade badly, as happens with weak individuals; if, however, one of them shows signs of ability in this new trade and, from being a Churchman, he shows himself capable in the use of his hands, shrewd in business, clever at dissimulation, a subtle schemer and so on, it will mean that his first vocation was the wrong one or, more precisely, it was not a vocation but an arbitrary social placement. Thus we sometimes ask ourselves, when faced with certain priests and friars, why they have dressed in that manner while their acts and their words assign to them a different role. And the same question comes to our lips in the face of certain philosophers, scientists, literary men, and teachers whom the events of life and certain secondary and superficial abilities have brought to these positions, which they would not defend in case of danger.

It is proved by history that the point of view of the " Church " or of ethics is superior to that of the " State " or of economics, since it is not possible to write a history of humanity which will be of all humanity and not of a partial and one-sided humanity, except as ethico-political history. Modern history has its origin in the *Historia ecclesiastica* founded by Christianity.[3]

---

[3] Cf. Croce, *Teoria e storia della storiografia*, pp. 189–190.

Chapter IX

INTERNATIONAL JUSTICE

IF we desire some point of meditation for understanding what is called the utilitarian or economico-political nature of the State, let us consider, for example, that whereas man as a moral being has, in certain given cases, the duty and the right to sacrifice his life, he has no such right over the life of the State. Even the man who is stirred by the most noble, fervid and daring ethical sentiment must, in any political capacity, act solely and wholeheartedly for the safety of the State, identifying himself completely with its welfare. Sometimes it will happen that he is forced to risk the existence or the prosperity of that State, but only because of the necessities arising from a struggle or in order to increase that State's power through bold undertakings. History does not acclaim as heroes those who have sacrificed their native land to an ideal, but rather condemns them for having subordinated the interests of the State to any other motive, however generous. In the comparison which he makes between the end of Carthage and the end of Gaul, between Hannibal and Vercingetorix, Mommsen tells us what we should think about kings and statesmen who behave like " knights " when they should have had recourse to cunning or, according to the Greek saying, to flight, because " he who flees will fight again."

These reflections serve to confirm that it is an error of logic to attempt to solve the moral problems of mankind by perverting the State and politics from their own nature, an error which opens the way to dangerous illusions or, in practice, to incongruous and harmful acts. And we can understand the so frequently shown diffidence, or at least the cautious reserve, toward international tribunals, leagues of nations, and toward the appeals to statesmen against the acts of oppression and the crimes that are committed in this or that part of the world. Because of the political nature of those institutions and those statesmen, as soon as the tribunals, the societies and the eagerly invoked measures begin to function, they are transformed into politics of the single States and produce effects that are at times only disappointing and deceiving, at times different from the dictates of the moral conscience, at times in conformity with these dictates, but operating not from moral considerations but from the interests of the strongest States or the most powerful unions. All these are things of which it is not necessary to cite examples.

And yet mankind does not renounce its longing and its demand for a more just, more gentle and more civilized world, that is, for a more human world, in which all rights will be protected; in which every good deed will find help and encouragement; in which hardships and sorrows will gradually diminish or will be transferred to a higher plane than that of cutting each other's throat; in which war will be abolished, not the metaphysical war which is inherent to life itself, but the war which continues the barbaric custom of bloodshed, massacres, cruelties and torments. Nor does mankind renounce its insistence and its hopes that the States will become the intermediaries and the instruments of this better world and will accept among their tasks and place above other tasks that of civilization, elevating themselves to " ethical States " or " States of culture." This civilization or culture is so closely bound up with the conditions prevailing throughout the entire world that it cannot be safeguarded or promoted except by an international policy, also based on civilization and culture.

Must we, if we accept this foregoing account, judge this impulse and working of the moral conscience to be useless and unfounded? This is not a logical deduction from those promises; if it were, so much the worse for them, because, in clashing in such a case with a very real and indestructible or constantly reappearing fact, they would expose their fallacy. The position is as we have stated, and at the same time this moral impulse and travail are sacred, which is tantamount to recognizing the truth of their theoretical basis. And not only are the two truths reconcilable between themselves, but, as is the case with all truths, the one finds its strength in the other, both combining in a greater truth.

In fact, the phase of the State and of politics is a necessary and eternal phase, but it is a phase and not the whole; and the moral conscience and activity is another phase, no less necessary and eternal, which follows the first, proceeding from and returning to spiritual unity. Certainly, if the second is indestructible, the first is no less indestructible; but this means simply that the second does not destroy the first, but instead exerts a perpetual influence on it, knocks perpetually at its door and perpetually makes itself heard and welcomed, yet conforming to the law which rules in that sphere. Thus poetry is not thought and philosophy; but philosophy and thought exert a perpetual influence on poetry and knock on its door and are welcomed by it, their voices time after time becoming modulated in poetry, in new poetry. In this continuous transformation of morals into politics, which still remains politics, lies the real ethical progress of mankind, just as in the transformation of thought into poetry lies the perfecting of an ever more rich and profound poetry. Thus on the one hand (in pure poetry) Homer, Dante, Shakespeare and Goethe are poets who cannot be compared with one another, and are independent of one another, on the other hand (in civil history) the one is placed in juxtaposition to the others in an ever-increasing spiritual complexity. Just as the poet, unconscious of philosophical concepts, finds his attitude of mind pervaded with new ideas, so the politician concentrating on utilitarian motives is confronted with new interests which arise from new moral needs, which he cannot evade and with which he must reckon; he must accept the new material with the old, just as he accepted the old, and must translate both alike into political action.

From the precise statement of this relation, which is badly defined or incorrectly presented by the political moralists (as, in the analogous case, by those who demand a directly philosophical poetry, which would not be poetry but a polemic or didactics), we derive the practical conclusion that it is not enough to call upon States and political men for works of moral value for the benefit of all mankind, loading on their shoulders the weight that should be carried by ours, asking of them efforts that should be made by us; but we must help them when necessary and meet them half way with the real changes effected in men's minds and hearts. Thus, we can say that it is not enough to request, but it is necessary to establish and impose the new situation which they will translate, according to the case, into laws, wars, treaties, and the like. If people could free their minds, by means of dispassionate research, of the foolish concepts of privileged races and nations and of perpetually hostile races and nations, and if, by making spirits more gentle, there could be an increase in the mutual sympathy between the various human families with their traditions and attitudes, which are traditions and attitudes of all mankind; how could the States and the men who govern their policy continue to follow those concepts and those prejudices and make use of them in their practical work, or increase their violence and virulence? The situation would demand a more humanitarian or more human policy : a policy toward which Europe seemed to be heading in the middle of the nineteenth century and from which it later gravely departed, until now Europe seems to be sailing very far from it, on a stormy sea, under dark skies. If respect for ideal and historical truth, for that life of thought which is one in all mankind, were to become more general, and if reflective and critical discernment and habit were to become more general, how could one help, in the face of the power exerted by this spiritual energy, pursuing a policy different from that which is pursued by daily creating false ideas, by playing on the imagination, and by confusing with empty words?

The negation, therefore, of the ethical character of the State as such has this among its motives : to take from superficial moralists the alibi which they discover for themselves when they busy themselves with asking States to change their nature and to practice morality, instead of attending on their own part to the serious duty of promoting the moral conscience and attitude in the world at large, in order that the States may always be confronted with them at every turn and help in serving them, without changing their own nature.

Chapter X

HISTORICAL PESSIMISM

THE shadow of pessimism covers from time to time the life of the individual and similarly the life of societies; and doubts, fears and despair over the future belongs to all eras of history. But, in the years through which Europe is living, that shadow has become wider and darker, and has produced a sombre literature, comprising books already famous, read by all or familiar to all. Philosophers, or people who call themselves philosophers, have become prophets and describe to us, under the guise of philosophical and historical reality, the steep incline we shall perforce descend or (an equally sad spectacle) the settlement which we shall have perforce to suffer.

It is a shadow that at times weighs heavily on the spirit and makes it weary, and at times, like a light fog, vanishes with a gust of wind, depending on how we take it and understand it.

When, as frequently happens, we conceive it as a tangle of forces which act outside us and according to their own laws, we have, with the nightmare of these forces, the feeling of helplessness, since, if they are outside us, there is no way of getting among them and of dominating or regulating them. There is nothing left to do then but to speculate, seeking in the external world other forces which may oppose, defeat or check them, and to put our hope in these. But it is an uncertain hope, always fearful, because it depends on others and not on us, and, whether fearful or hopeful, we feel in the clutch of others. Many judgments and presentiments of which we see daily manifestations follow this pattern. For example, there are the opinions and emotions about the Asiatic peril, which will pour upon little Europe overpowering waves of Turanian peoples, awakened and directed by bolshevism. We find relief from this peril in the thought that those peoples will remain closed in their boundaries and will not become either communists or nationalists according to European concepts. Or we have the judgments and presentiments about the fatality of communism, which will make European life uniformly coarse and poor, giving rise to dictatorships and authoritarian forms of government, to bureaucracy and Byzantinism, and preparing a new barbarism. We find relief from this peril too, by thinking of the forces of resistance still found in some European countries, and by thinking of the unextinguished feeling for one's own fatherland and ancestry, and the like. Or, again, there are judgments and presentiments about the historical and religious era upon which we shall enter, one that is not produced by our thought ancient or modern, but imposed on us by the course of events, as a spiritual victory of the Orient over the Occident. Against this we reflect that Brahmanism and Buddhism will not prevail against our religions and philosophies, which already have in them the elements of those and other religions, but criticized and subdued. In the end, in spite of comforting arguments, we are left with fear and worry.

But when, on the other hand, we do not accept this view of the situation, nor, consequently, this manner of stating the problem; when we retain or awaken the consciousness that history is what we make it, and that all the rest does not concern us, for the good reason that in reality it does not exist; when we return to a true perspective, that oppressive weight is no longer felt, that dark cloud becomes tattered and disappears, and there reappear in us faith, peace of mind, security, and enthusiasm for our work.

Actually, these imaginings which we project into the future with the reality of powerful forces are taken from the records of history, invested with a rigid material form and, through these, transfer to the future, furnished with a threatening appearance. Can these things happen again, if not exactly as they were in the past—since nothing is repeated—in a similar or analogous manner? Everything can happen, but in this everything is included also its opposite. Wherefore, with this fine thought, we get nowhere. Can these fears at least be useful as scarecrows? Hardly, since by giving them such a name we hold them up to scorn and derision. Can they be useful as possibilities to be kept in mind, as risks which we are facing? But there are risks in every act of life, and therefore we always keep in mind adverse possibilities and sharpen our intellect to perceive clearly the reality in the midst of which we act.

The attitude here recommended may seem over-simple; perhaps it should be integrated by giving men the proper advice to guide them victoriously through their trials. But this is precisely what one is always trying to do, to the best of one's knowledge and ability. Would it be helpful if prophets should arise to awaken spirits and to lead the masses. It would be helpful; but neither the yearning for prophets nor caricatures of prophets would be of any use. Should we hope that the world may be thrilled by sayings that unite people spiritually, similar to that heard at the close of the eleventh century, " God wills it "? Certainly, it would be a fine thing; but even to-day there are sayings which unite people, quite a lot of them, and richer in content than that one. In short, once we have found the true centre, we must not go slipping again toward the outside, and treat our own spirit as a force to be influenced by more or less external means. The problem is always purely one of knowledge and will; and there are no remedies which can take the place of the intellectual and moral consciousness, or that can be of help to that consciousness unless it can help itself.

THE END

For Product Safety Concerns and Information please contact our EU
representative GPSR@taylorandfrancis.com
Taylor & Francis Verlag GmbH, Kaufingerstraße 24, 80331 München, Germany

www.ingramcontent.com/pod-product-compliance
Lightning Source LLC
Chambersburg PA
CBHW050718280326
41926CB00088B/3198

9 780367 143701